The Private Haystack

Yolanda D. Logan

The Private Haystack

Copyright@ 2018

ISBN #978-0-692-98309-6

All rights reserved.

Note: Printed in the United States of America by 'Createspace.'
For more information on the author see www.Amazon.com

DEDICATION

In loving memory of Evangelist Lulu Belle ("Granny") Pervoich, who discovered a sense of duty, purpose, and responsibility in spreading the gospel.

&

For those who also routinely practice the art of forgiveness.

ACKNOWLEDGEMENTS

AMAZON

&

The Fred Jordan's Los Angeles Mission, Los Angeles, CA; a non-profit organization

The Humane Society of the United States; a non-profit organization

The Salvation Army, San Francisco, CA; a non-profit organization

Wikimedia Foundation; a non-profit organization

&

The City of Berkeley California (BPD)

The City of Los Angeles Police Department (LAPD)

The City of Oakland Police Department (OPD)

GOD bless the United States of America, our active military, veterans, allies, as well as family and friends by 'The Bay.'

A Message to the Readers

Similar to other authors, for a few months, off and on, I was struggling with creating a title for this book. Early summer of 2017, I finally settled on, "The Private Haystack," and reflectively thought, 'I hope it's relatable.' Notably, I'm one of the 76.4 million Baby Boomers born in the United States. Gratefully, I've also reached a point, where I can actually shop on a weekday, rather than the traditional jam-packed weekend.

On September 18, 2017, at 8:10 a.m., I was still somewhat sleepy, and my inner spirit faintly asked, 'Why don't you lie down for another hour or so?' Admittedly, as I'm advancing through life, I've been focusing on listening more profoundly. Since I wasn't in a hurry, I readily complied. Later, around 12 noon, returning from Martinez, on CA 4, heading westbound, (a local highway, surrounded by pockets of farmland, and inspirational mountains); I found myself reminiscing with jazz vocalist Al Jarreau's song entitled, 'Something That You Said,' as well as pondering over the staggering number of homeless folks marginally surviving in one of the wealthiest regions in the country - the San Francisco Bay Area.

Out of the blue, I pulled behind a classic, sky blue, 1955 Studebaker pickup truck (not fully restored); with 'S-T-U-D-E-B-A-K-E-R,' stenciled in thin, tall, white letters featured on its tailgate; along with a mature male driver at the wheel. Interestingly, he was hauling four bundles of hay. Fairly amused, by such a timely occurrence, I thought, 'How ironic... So that's why it was suggested to remain in bed a little longer. If I had departed sooner, I certainly would've missed him,' (Dad previously owned a 50's something white Studebaker sedan). Clearly, the noted episode doesn't sound like much. There's no mayhem or murder to speak of. However, as a true believer, such occurrence was considered insightful. Lastly, in the final analysis, it also hinted that no matter how this book is regarded, at least, I chose the correct title.

Thank you for reading.

Table of Contents

Introduction

Glossary

INTRODUCTION

Early autumn 2017, on a humid and windy Thursday morning, prospective passengers were patiently waiting in a rather long and solitary security line at The Hollywood Burbank Airport, located in Burbank California. Seemingly, a refined, charming, easy going, male stranger, wearing a tailored grey suit ensemble, with meticulously combed, wavy silver hair, appropriately stooped down, and removed one of his matching, Italian, leather shoes, "Don't forget to remove yours," he kindly advised. "Stop. Are we still doing that?" Southern Crest Police Department (SCPD), Vice Detective II, Harriet ("Harri") Wilburn half-jokingly asked. "I'm afraid so. You'll also need to take off your belt," he replied as he elevated his head and took note of it.

Captivated by his debonair appearance, seamless coordination, exquisite fragrance, and a classy diamond ring placed on his left pinky, she stimulatingly thought, *'Oooh wee, a real lady's man.'* In hindsight, *'Or a pro.'* In particular, Harri is a brunette in her mid-40s, with shoulder length hair, and willowy bangs. Noticeably, she possesses an apple shaped body; with tiny brown freckles arbitrarily scattered across her nose; and due to her darken cheek bones, it implied that her complexion had been overexposed. She also has an aged occupational scar, prominently featured across her right knuckles. On such occasion, she was tastefully dressed in a tan, silk blended blouse, and dark brown corduroy pants.

In addition, she also wore a multi-earth colored scarf, which was adorned around her neck; an enviable suede almond colored jacket, along with a matching belt, and laced up crew boots; as well as a small lovely pair of white gold, dew drop earrings, and a stylish wrist watch. Since she doesn't generally fuss over makeup, she applied a relatively carefree foundation, her favorite rustic colored lipstick, easy on the brown eyeliner, and some SPF 50+ sunscreen. Contrary to what many travelers wore, Harri was considered appropriately dressed, especially, since her destination commonly embraced all four seasons. By chance, she was heading home.

Despite such superficial imperfections, she exudes confidence, possesses a genuine warm smile, as well as an engaging and humorous personality. It should also be duly noted that she has a *Type A'* personality. Nonetheless, on such morning, she was visibly favoring her left leg. Within moments, the line halted, and she thought, *'Good. That'll give me a chance to look at this darn boot. Why does the left feel tighter than the right? I know our feet grow, but not one at a time. At least, I don't think so. Perhaps, my size seven and a half, somehow became mixed up with an eight. How did that happened?'*

While outgoing passengers were waiting, some began casually chatting with each other. Specifically, one short, portly, young fella, with dark spiky hair; who wore black frame eyeglasses, and a garish green tee-shirt that read, *'Check the Rear,'* turned to a female stranger, "Hey, I heard they're considering cavity searches.

I'll volunteer, if it'll solve my weekly battle with constipation," he jokingly said. "While they're doing their business, I'll serenade, 'Down in the valley, the valley so low, hang your head over hear the wind blow...' Smacking on some fruity chewing gum, "Are you even liked?" she sarcastically asked. "Completed surveys are pouring in as we speak." "Seriously, I'm from East Flatbush." "Duh?" Rolling her eyes, "The Bronx, you dimwit. Listen, if any buster tries to exam my voluptuous keister, he'll find these five inch stilettos up his cha-chas," an audacious Puerto Rican female confidently conveyed, as she flaunted her black heels.

Within a short period, the line started moving again, and everyone began placing all of their personal items such as keys, wallets, loose change, shoes, into the allotted gray tote boxes. During such transition, Harri took a chance and snatched off the troubling boot, "Geez, we're moving again. I'll never be able to look inside," she frustratingly griped as she hobbled forward. Acknowledging her discontent, the well-groomed stranger tossed his wallet and keys into the container, peeked over his shoulders and said, "At 5:10 in the morning, there's nothing wrong with passengers running into a brief snag or two, as long as no one misses their flight."

Unfastening his belt, "Let doubt and fear be the other guy's problem," he added with a sly wink. Strengthen by his expressed beliefs, she stopped dead in her tracks, and attempted to inspect the interior label. "What's going on up there? .....Ahh, c'mon lady!" a male voice shouted. Whirling around, "Shut Up Big Mouth! I haven't flown in a while!"

"Whose problem is that?? DO WE ALL HAVE TO SUFFER??!!" he maddeningly countered from the back of the line. Squinting at the small white tag, she began speedily patting her jacket pockets, *'Wouldn't you know it? I left my reading glasses at home. This day is starting off splendid,'* she anxiously thought. Swiftly, she removed her other boot, and hurled them into the gray tote. Once she approached the checkpoint, a young, fair-haired, female dressed in a tight, wool, blue uniform, who deliberately wore her badge upside down, motioned her into the full body scanner, "Step onto the yellow shoes prints," she aptly requested.

Immediately thereafter, a full figured, Creole, female Security Officer, with auburn hair; a recent transferee from Shreveport, Louisiana; properly patted her chest, "Ma'am, you have something solid underneath your blouse. Please remove it." Without delay, she dug into her blouse, and pulled on a silver chain, which held her Police badge. Promptly, she showed the shiny metal, and returned it, "I'm Detective Harriet Wilburn with SCPD (Southern Crest Police Department).

Currently, I'm working on a special assignment with LAPD (Los Angeles Police Department)..." she partially whispered. "Don't you dare wave your funky drawers in my face!" she radically screamed with a distinctive twang. Spontaneously, a bunch of looky-loos crazily jumped out of line. Situated somewhere in the middle, with an obstructed view, "WHOA! Some chick just flashed her panties!" a husky voice bellowed. "No way!" a nonbeliever shouted. Twisting around, "I saw them!" a young man easily fabricated. "It happened lightning fast! She unzipped her pants, then BAM!

Seconds later, she shut the fortress! They're pinkish!" "How nasty!" an elderly Korean woman shrieked. "Dang!" a young African American male energetically yelled. "Woo, I missed that! That's my favorite color! C'mon baby, let's play some more show and tell!" others animatedly echoed. Tapping on the shoulders of a male stranger, and demonstrating with her dainty hands, "Señor, perdón ("Sir, pardon me"). Um, could you tell if they have these beautiful peach angel wings hanging on each side?" a petite Hispanic female intriguingly asked.

With no response provided, "Oooh, I wonder if she bought them from *Para Los Atrevidos Boutique Mujer ('For the Daring Woman Boutique')*?" she said as she stood on her tippy toes attempting to view the commotion. Meanwhile another stranger dramatically dropped his brown, canvas, carry-on bag, "Are you happy?" he derisively asked his female companion. "Now we'll be here forever. I warned you. This would've never happened, if we connected in Los Angeles or San Francisco. Someone is always screwing around in Hollywood!"

While their backs were somewhat facing the crowd, "I hope you ain't some heathen, toting steel," she annoyingly insinuated while patting her thighs, legs, and ankles. Physically agitated, "What kind of (expletive) Betty Boob are you??" Harri fired back. Suddenly, the Security Officer cocked her head, spun around, and gawked at the crowd, "HEY!! What are you varmints staring at?? Ya'll better get back in line, or ain't none of ya'll boarding nothing!!" she hostilely ordered. Instantly, everyone madly scrambled to their original positions, except two men.

Strangely, gawking at his grandson, "Varmints? That's insulting. Who does she think she is? This isn't a cattle call for the wild, wild, west, you know," an elderly Jewish gentleman gruffly remarked. Gingerly, escorting his grandfather back in line, "Saba, she's the gatekeeper. If you don't want us to dine on cold cheese sandwiches tonight, we better do as she says," he sensibly urged.

Resuming their heated discussion, "Where were we? Oh, yes. Listen up, Miss Rootin-Tootin. Despite your sourpuss disposition, I have you know that we instruct all of our passengers to adhere to the same exact procedures." Sharply, fingering her duty belt, "You see this? My high powered flashlight is far more critical than you. Now could you remove all items from your person, and place them into the tray? Don't let me ask you again!" she strongly stated. With a wide eyed expression, "I was only trying to be discreet," she murmured. "Missy, your germy, smelly, bathroom is specially designed for that purpose. Up in here, we're only interested in full disclosure. You know the drill! Don't act coy! NEXT!!" she hollered while motioning another.

Chapter 1

Bungled the Birds & the Bees Session

As expected, Harri fearlessly stood her ground and failed to proceed. "You're still here?" the Security Officer bizarrely questioned. Scanning the perimeter, "I tried to be respectful, but who in the *%@#^% is your supervisor?" she angrily asked. "Don't look too far baby cakes." "Oops." "If you don't move within ten seconds, I'll bounce you for a ton of FAA and TSA violations. Am I making myself crystal clear? Or do you need a pair of stainless steel bracelets to make you feel warm and cozy?" she brutally asked.

"Boss lady, I don't know what you've been snorting on, but this isn't over by a long shot!" Without hesitation, the Supervisor raised her chin, hastily dug into her blouse, retrieved a referee whistle, blew twice, and summoned two robust Security Officers from a distance, "Fellas, we've got a live one!" Fiercely, marching in her direction, *'Uh-oh. They're carrying those plastic zip-tie handcuffs. Oooh, I hate those, their scratchy,'* she intensely thought.

Swiftly, she gathered her belongings, carelessly slipped on and tied her boots, and held her badge high into the air. "Sorry, this was a huge misunderstanding. I'm a SCPD Peace Officer! It'll never happen again!" she desperately pleaded. "Alright fellas, let her go! And let this be a lesson to you! Cause nobody messes with Creebie's Baby-Mama!" she rowdily shouted. "Yes, ma'am!"

Scurrying into a nearby lounge, she quickly plopped into a comfy leather chair. Pondering over recent events, *'What a mess! Geez! It's not even six o' clock, and I was almost arrested by a couple of bayou trappers. Why is my life turning into a virtual crap sandwich? Besides all of that, lately, I've met the most inadequate prospects. They run the gamut from married with children, committed womanizers; habitual divorcees, harden criminals, too young and inexperienced, to momma's boys.*

Speaking of which, what's up with Brock (partner)? Is he sleeping with a hooker? Ugh! None of my beeswax. Why doesn't he shut off his computer at the end of the day like everybody else? Now I remember why I hate flying. It gives me plenty of time to think, and I don't need that. And those (expletives) security guards expects everyone to tap dance on demand. Geez, no one has respect anymore,' she uneasily thought.

Slumping over and removing each boot, she fluctuated from squinting to widening her eyes, and retracting her arms back and forward, in an effort to read the interior tags. Becoming highly frustrated, she keenly observed a smartly dressed businessman, who fortuitously was wearing a pair of wired frame eyeglasses, while contentedly reading the morning newspaper. In a flash, she scampered over, stood next to him, and dangled one boot near the side of his face, "Say buddy, do me a favor? Tell me what these labels say," she boldly asked.

Completely stunned, with his mouth partly opened, he gradually lowered his material, "You realize, you're also compelling me to inhale," he said in a sterile manner. "C'mon, it'll only take a second."

"Make it quick." Promptly, she displayed both tags, and he turned up his nose, "I see your problem. One is a size seven and a half, and the other an eight," he said. Returning to the "Metro" section, "You and my ex have something in common." "What is that?" she plainly asked. "She also thought the attractive but cheap was worth the effort," he snootily replied." Returning to her chair, "And you're nothing but a horrid piece of window dressing," she said under her breath. *'Riggs, #$@&%^, swapped one of my old boots, with a new one. I married a moron. I can't wait until he finish moving out,'* she thought.

[Cell phone rang], "This is Harri." "Hey mom," Nathan said. "Hi, I'm at Burbank Airport heading for San Francisco. Did you see the note I left on the refrigerator?" she asked. "Um hum. For the next two days, you're going to be at the Oakland Police Department's downtown division. You'll be home tomorrow evening." "Is everything alright?" she asked. "Yeah, no worries. I'm just calling to tell you that Linda is pregnant." "Who's that?" "My girlfriend, mom. C'mon, you know her." "I've met several. At least a dozen in the past two years. Didn't you attend high school with a bright girl named Linda Fong?" "Yeah." "She would've never gotten pregnant until she was married."

"Wow! You know, I'm mean Linda Barnett," he said with a chuckle. "No such luck, huh? You're only twenty, and you don't know the first clue about raising a child." "Dad was only twenty six, when you guys had me," he countered. "That's a huge six year difference. Besides your father and I were married, and we were holding down full-time jobs."

"What's behind a number anyway?" he defensively questioned. "Ooh, I don't know. Try a stable home, decent savings account, medical insurance, and a few significant life experiences tucked under your belt. Did you even try keeping your ping pong locked up a little longer?" she agonizingly asked. "There's always a safer option." "Like I'm going to discuss that with you. I know it's hard to imagine, but I'm not a boy anymore," he asserted. "You got me there. So how far along is she?" "She don't know."

"Are you certain she's pregnant?" she skeptically inquired. "We're sure. She already took two pregnancy tests; one at home, and yesterday, at the clinic. But Linda isn't sure about how many months. She missed her period at least two or three times. Um, I think. During her appointment, the doctor told her that she was three. But what does he know? He wasn't there. We'll figured it out," he indifferently replied. "Correct me, if I'm wrong. When you were thirteen, didn't your father have a closed door, heart-to-heart talk with you concerning the birds and the bees? I also recalled him walking into your bedroom with a super-size box of condoms," she said.

"Yeah. He also brought in some root beer, pretzel sticks, and a newspaper. For a few minutes, he explained how to properly inspect and place on a condom. Then, we got down to the nitty gritty, and checked the internet for the NFL's (National Football League), draft results." "He was in there for quite some time, wasn't he?" "Um hum." "Help me understand. He spent a whopping ten minutes discussing one of the most important topics of your young life, and the other hour and a half was dedicated to football?"

"Um, it was more like five minutes chatting about condoms, and two hours bickering over our picks. We were trying to figure out who was right," he clarified. "He should've devoted the majority of his time explaining human nature; when you're considered sexually mature; and by all means, emphasized the importance of abstinence." "That wasn't necessary. I already knew everything, but I didn't want to make him feel bad. So I let him go for it." "Whatever happened to the box? If I'm not mistaken, there were over a hundred inside." "What box?" "The box of condoms," she replied with a sigh.

Chuckling out loud, "Those been gone," he flatly answered. "Have you purchased anymore?" "Yeah, I'm not stupid. But they're not nearly the same quality as the ones Dad gave me. Usually, I'll pick up some from the swap meet – three for a buck. Say, you think if I ask him to buy me some more, he'll do it?" he sheepishly asked. "Not that I really need them, right now." "No, Nate, that's your responsibility." "Since we're on the subject I figured, no harm, no foul." "I can't believe your father. What an egghead. No wonder we're getting a divorce," she murmured. "What?" "Never mind."

"Hey, I'm glad you brought this up. I forgot, he still owes me a ten spot. I'm going to text him. I could use the dough." "I knew I should've been in that meeting, but he said, *'This conversation is strictly for men.'* " "Dad was right. You don't know squat about football. You would've been bored stiff." "Uh-huh. So I take it Linda doesn't use contraceptives?" "She has been on the pill for a while. So we thought we didn't have to worry. Though, somedays she would forget.

Clyde, a friend of mines at work, told me they're not full proof, anyway," he naively responded. Covering the speaker, 'Only if she's not taking them as prescribed,' she uttered. "Whew! Nate, let's table this conversation until I get home. I don't want to miss my flight." "Cool." "Don't forget to feed Grady (a black Labrador retriever with a large white spot in the center of his chest), before you leave for work, and stick to his feeding schedule that's posted on the fridge," she reinforced.

"Oh, and don't let him bully you. He's into that these days." "Dad and I believe that he got that from you," he said with a snicker. "What a compliment." "Anyway, I'm off today." "How nice." "I was planning on mixing a little chicken salad with his dry food. He loves that stuff." "I believe it's the mayonnaise, which potentially isn't good for him. Please don't give him too much, he's spoiled enough," she said. "Since he stayed out of hot water this week, yesterday, I promised him that we would go hiking, this morning."

"Sounds like fun. Where?" "Skully's Ridge. But I'm postponing it, until Dad wakes up. Last night, he texted me and said he's going with us." "It gets really hot out there. If you guys are going to stay over an hour, take a backpack." "We're both taking one. Um, I need to ask you a question, but it can wait. Hey, the next time you go shopping, could you let Linda or her Mom know if you spot any deals on baby clothes?" he asked. "What?" "Bye, Grandma!" ['Click'].

Squeezing her bottom lip, *That confirms it, I have a goofball for a son. I bet Riggs knew. I guess I should contact her parents, or is that appropriate these days?*

Oh boy, they're way too immature to become parents, and I'm much too young to become a grandmother. Nate doesn't realize he's living in a money grab society. He better stop spending so much on his cell. Gosh, I hope he doesn't ask if they could they live with me,' she thought.

Forty minutes later, the dark skies were beautifully transitioning into a glorious sunrise, and all of the scheduled passengers began boarding United Airlines, (UA's Boeing 777 aircraft), 7:00 a.m. flight, #1916, heading for San Francisco. Hovering over Southern California at a comfortable altitude of around 39,000 feet, Harri was sitting in row 37, seat A (a window seat); wearing a headset, and digging Peter White's (jazz guitarist) song entitled, *'Don't wait for me.' Taking* in the magnificent aerial view, she thought, *'You really gain some perspective up here. Our country's landscape is spectacular. There's nothing like it. Whether you're the richest man in the world, you're surely reminded that we're all speckles of dust, taking our turn, twirling on the ground. Hum, I should check with the Crenshaw unit, and see if any additional information came in on our perp.'*

Thereafter, she retrieved her cellphone, hit speed dial #8, and an unfamiliar voice exuberantly rapped, "Good morning, and many blessing to you and yours. This is Peace Officer Jamal Kareem Abdullah Hassan Muhammad at your service. If you're inquiring about our bean pie special, we're extending it for another month. So don't wait or hesitate, get your bean pie, before it's too late!" *'Un (expletive) believable,'* she wearily thought. With a moment of silence, "Is this Mr. Chee's?" he readily presumed.

"This is Detective Harriet Wilburn with SCPD. Is this some sort of joke, or is this LAPD?" "Who told you?" he playfully asked. Immediately thereafter, she checked the outbound listed number, "Okay Muhammad or whoever you are. I'm on a flight heading for San Francisco. So cut the crap," she heatedly conveyed. "Where's your sense of humor Detective Harri? You don't remember me, do you? I'm Jamal. I'm 6'8, African American, one of the tallest officers within SCPD." "Um, um, yes, I remember you." "Last week, I was assigned to assist with the joint task force, patrol section. However, today, since Officer Williams called in sick, they requested that I cover the special phone lines. Over a month ago, we ran into you and your partner at Pedro's Mexican Restaurant.

At the time, I was working as part of Deputy Chief Hall's security detail," he explained. "Yea, yea, but why are you answering with a sales spiel? Then, asking about Mr. Chee's? Officer Muhammad, that's so (expletive) unprofessional. I hope no one from LAPD gets wind of your nonsensical babbling. If they do, they'll be giving us all the boot," she growled. "With all due respect, the Crenshaw station is currently pushing bean pies for the upcoming Thanksgiving holiday season. Our campaign has drummed up a lot of goodwill within this community, and all of the proceeds are going to the Fred Jordan's Los Angeles Mission. Since we're here on temporary assignment, they've also requested that we assist the 77th and Southwest Divisions with their efforts. So far, we've been selling bean pies like hotcakes.

Yesterday, in our morning briefing, Lieutenant Kim advised that starting next week, their Central and Rampart Divisions will be adding apple, cherry, pecan, and sweet potato to the list. *['Click, Click']*. Shoot! Did you hear that? Call back Detective! That's Mr. Chee's! T.J. forgot to order wonton soup along with the Captain's order. Heads will roll, if he doesn't get it," he excitedly declared [*'Click'*]. Nodding in disbelief, *'I can appreciate his enthusiasm, but he shouldn't be answering the telephone in that manner. Hum, if I was to call back, and ask to speak with the department's supervisor, I'll be portrayed as the bad guy. Forget it,' she thought.* Seconds later, she possessed a puzzled look, *'Why did I call?'*

Then, she came up with a familial idea, and contacted Carol, her younger sister. After a few short rings, "Hello." "Did I wake you?" "No, I've been up since 3:00. I'm at work. Are you okay?" she asked. "Um hum. I'll keep it brief. What do you have planned for today?" "Nothing much. I'm off at 11:30 a.m." "Great. I'm on a plane heading to San Francisco. Yesterday evening, one of our suspects fled our jurisdiction, was later apprehended and placed in custody by OPD (Oakland Police Department)."

"You're flying alone?" she curiously inquired. "Um hum. Brock, my partner, had ants in his pants. So he flew up there last night. Hey, since we haven't seen each other in a while, I thought we could catch up. How about lunch or an early dinner?" she asked. "Whenever. I'm available. Has it been a year?" "Sounds right." "I wish Bonnie wasn't in school. I know she would love to see her Aunt Harri. Funny, she just mentioned you the other day.

What time do you want to meet?" "Noonish. By then, we should have everything wrapped up. Are we good?" "Yes." "See you." ['Click']. Near the approximate time, Carol retrieved a load of clothes from the dryer. As usual, she dumped, sorted, and folded them on the living room couch. Midway, she checked her wristwatch, *'Should I call her? No, I'll wait. She'll get in touch with me,'* she thought.

Chapter 2

<u>Who In The Heck Is Mary Jane?</u>

At approximately 1:15 p.m., Harri called, "Sorry for the delay. It took a little longer than I expected. We weren't certain if the suspect that OPD is holding, was the perp we were looking for." "Is he?" Carol asked. "Yep! Once he dropped his pants, we were able to positively identify him," she replied. "Drop his pants?" "Hearing it repeated, does sound weird. In a nutshell, three days ago, we conducted a raid on an abandoned warehouse. He and several others were running a one stop shop." "I should know what that means," she mumbled. "They were manufacturing, packaging, and distributing heavy drugs. Somehow our perp escaped and landed in OPD's territory," she explained.

"Okay, I got that. But I don't understand why he had to lower his pants?" "According to our witness and his pissed off ex-girlfriend, who also tipped us on his potential whereabouts, they both claimed he has a tattoo that features a woman's head with a leopard's body, located below the tan line." "Near his hiney?" "Three inches from his right cheek." "What an imagination." "You haven't heard nothing yet." "What does he look like?" she intriguingly asked. "He's a fresh, twenty four year old, not a bad looking dude, with no prints, and doesn't give a rat (expletive) about shooting people." "He's so young." "Most of them are." "Does he have a street name?" "Um hum. It's sloppy." "C'mon, I assume he's sloppy, all kids are," Carol quipped. "No, that's his street name – Sloppy. Unreal, I know. According to OPD, the suspect says he's not the guy."

"Did he shoot someone?" "Um hum. A runner during a dicey exchange." "Did he confess?" "Boy, you've been watching too many reruns of Perry Mason," she responded with a chuckle. "By the way, did you name my nephew after him?" she asked. "No, after Eugene's (husband) grandfather." "To answer your question, those guys don't fess up unless there's a favorable deal on the table, and we haven't reach that point yet." "Did he at least cooperate and show his tattoo?" she enquired. "Only in our dreams, and once he lawyered up, everything became more convoluted. While we were waiting for a court order, and his greasy lawyer, things got heated between him and Brock," she replied. "Why?"

"My partner made the mistake of mentioning how tired and hungry he was. And the perp said, *'Say man, grab me a Reuben and a coke, and I'll tip you large before I skip out.'* That set off a swearing war. Needless to say, some vicious threats were being slung around. Actually, it was entertaining watching two grown men cursing at each other. They also reference their doting moms," she strangely responded. "How disrespectful." "You had to be there, it was humorous. Regrettably, I was duty bound to break it up. Then, I cuffed the (expletive) to the table. Suddenly, Brock smacked the wall and shouted, *'Why do we have to obtain a warrant? This is ridiculous! The %#$@^* is right here! Hey, why don't you cut us some slack? You (expletive)!'*

Giggling out loud, "Like he should care whether you guys ever eat again," Carol remarked. "Oooh, and Brock wanted us to go to this popular chili house for lunch, somewhere in Oakland. But I despise beans."

"What kind?" "Whatever kind they're serving." "I don't want to sidetrack too much, before I finish telling you about bonehead." "Go ahead." "When we exited the interview room, I inquired about his ridiculous request, and he said, *'I was appealing to his sense of compassion.'* Then, I noticed he was wearing something extremely loud underneath his white dressed shirt. So I asked, *'What's glowing?'* Immediately, he unbuttoned and loosened it up, and crazily replied, *'Ta-da! I know what you're thinking. I told her it didn't match my eyes. But I promised to wear it today.'*"

"What was it?" "It was a hot pink tank top that read, *Sexy Dada!*" she disgustingly responded. "What did you say?" *'Where in the hell did you get that?'* "And what did he say?" *'From Mary Jane.'* "Who? I don't quite follow you. That's an old-fashioned name. By chance, is the lady a hooker?" "Smells that way, doesn't it?" "OMG, Brock is dating a hooker!" "Hypothetically, let's say, that he has an arrangement. In any case, I need to speak with him further. I hope he's not changing into a 5150," she said with a snicker. "I'm familiar with that term, and he's nowhere near being escorted to the loony bin." "I forgot you work in the medical profession." "Yes, so don't be silly."

"We'll keep this info on the down low." "Hum?" "Mums the word." "Gotcha." "I just have a couple of other questions." "Shoot." "Why didn't you chat with him right then and there?" she inquired. "Flynn, one of OPD's Detectives, was snooping around his satchel. He didn't know who it belonged to. These days, you can never be too careful. So Brock rushed over."

"Going back to your investigation, how long did it take to obtain a warrant?" she asked. "We were lucky, only three hours. Once obtained, of course, Brock felt overly compelled to assist our suspect with lowering his pants and undies. This was one of those rare moments, when I wished I was in another profession. As you can imagined, the perp's (expletive) butt cheek had to be examined." "Oooh, that's classic!" "For a moment, I thought for kicks, he was going to pee on the floor. His mind is that warp." "EW!" "We were also required to snap a photo. Since I didn't want any part of it, Brock conducted the entire inspection," she said. "You have to admit your suspect was creative."

"You could call it that. Right now, our buddies at OPD have him under wraps. Tomorrow, he'll be traveling with us, along with his smutty behind." "One final question – what crime did he allegedly commit?" she inquired. "He was slanging." "Slinging? Gun slinging?" "No slanging." "Slanging? I give." "He was primarily responsible for making the connections as well as selling the heavy drugs," she responded.

"I know we've tossed around this topic countless times. But why do you enjoy your job? The only reason I'm asking is because every story you've shared is grimy, and you're continually interacting with depraved individuals. You received good grades in high school. Why don't you attend college at night, and study for another career?" she suggested. "First, despite my complaints, I'm darn good at what I do. Secondly, have you retired your push-up bra? I'm too old to be going back to school, and then, starting a new low paying position. Trust me, I'm fine," she answered.

"Are good paying jobs still hard to come by in Los Angeles County?" "You better believe it." "That's too bad. Hopefully, the economy will improve soon. Where do you want to meet?" she asked. "Prior to leaving the office, one of the guys brought in some breakfast burritos, and I split one with Brock. So I'm not hungry," she answered. "At 10:00 o'clock, I had a banana, oatmeal, two slices of raisin toast, and some orange juice. Say, let's step out for some tea?" Carol recommended. "Straight black for me. How about *Far Out?* They serve a variety of beverages." "I don't want to be sipping, while watching some kids going berserk on those silly arcade machines. Anyway, it's no longer located in Berkeley. I believe Duke relocated his center to San Jose."

"Really?" "Um, hum." "Gosh, you're such a liar! Have you ever thought of going into politics? If Mister Man ever decides to move his business, at a minimum, he would send me a smoke signal. His place is a gold mine. You just don't care for the atmosphere." "I knew you possessed other talents. You're also a mind reader," she jokingly said. "And you should consider running for mayor in your teeny tiny town," Harri countered with a laugh. "Perhaps, after I retire." "Um hum." "In July, Mason finally left for college. Naturally, I miss him. But I could bypass seeing him, and his high school buddies together again."

"Why?" "Whenever they came over, they were all sweet darlings – *'Hi Mrs. Miller.'* Once they entered his bedroom/man cave, the noise level would swing from pleasant chatter to outrageous roars. I was never certain whether something was dreadfully wrong, or if they were simply fooling around.

It was definitely time for all of them to be carted off to college," she rationalized. "I know what you mean. Sometimes kids can become a little rowdy." "After New Year's, I'm planning on converting his cave into a fitness room." "Does he know?" "Um hum. Anyway, I lied, because Mason's old room reminds me of *'Far Out,'* she explained. "Besides leaving his boyhood memories, how's he doing?" she asked. Sounding somewhat reluctant, "This is considered a post discussion. I should've told you earlier." "What is it?" "Mason has multiple girlfriends." "How many?" "Six." "Why?" "I've asked him several times. For the longest, he couldn't or wouldn't give me a straight answer. Then, one day, he laughed it off, and said, *'It's less complicated, no attachments.'*

In the past three months, I've spoken with two angry parents regarding this matter. One of the girls went into a deep state of depression, and had to be hospitalized." "Did you tell Eugene?" she asked. "Yes, and he said, *'He's a young man sowing his wild oats.'* "Uh-uh, that's not the right attitude to have," Harri determined. "Tell me about it. I didn't raise him to disrespect women," she unwaveringly stated. "Um hum, I know." "Mason was raised in the faith with solid Christian values. He wasn't brought up to behave like an untamed, wild animal, perpetually in heat. One way or another, I'm afraid GOD will severely punish him for emotionally hurting those girls."

"Life is challenging enough, without pissing off the big guy," Harri murmured. "I'm also concerned that he's increasing his chances of contracting a venereal disease. Where did I go wrong?" she sadly asked. "Association brings on simulation.

Were you and Eugene closely screening his friends? We did." "No." "It helps. Nate previously had a couple of shifty pals visit one time, and I told him that they couldn't come over any more. Initially, he became upset and defensive, but he knew he couldn't buck our rules." "So you put your foot down." "We both did." "I didn't think it wouldn't have made a difference, especially, since he would've eventually saw them at hockey practice, school, or visited their homes," she said. "It's just setting standards, that's all. In terms of contracting a disease, I suppose it depends on his level of sexual activity. You should consult with your family doctor." "I'll do that."

"I've been meaning to ask you, did you resign from? Um, what's the name of your employer?" "It's called, *'Shaky Parts Medical Clinic.'* No, I decided to stay a while longer. Don't forget to bring it up when we meet, and I'll give you the inside scoop." "See you within an hour?" she presumed. "Um hum, but you owe me." Forty five minutes later, Harri was strolling by an array of artsy vendors on Telegraph Avenue in Berkeley, California. In particular, one young man, with peach fuzz sprinkled on his chin, unexpectedly shoved a small sandwich bag of cannabis within her reach, "Lady, you look like your back is aching," he loosely insinuated. "What?" "Won't you stop by my shop? Then, I'll fire up a blunt, and we'll ease those tight muscles in no time. It's legal," he convincingly replied.

Impulsively, she slid her right hand down her blouse, pulled out her SCPD badge, and leaned forward, "Dude, you can't solicit folks off the streets," she advised. Strolling away, *'I should contact BPD (Berkeley Police Department),'* she thought.

"Hey Cutie Pie!" he shouted with his hands cupped around his mouth. "We shouldn't care about what each other does to make our bread!! Want to go out tonight??" he boldly shouted. *'His act belongs in a Comedy Club. He's close to Nate's age,'* she amusingly thought. "I REALLY DIG OLDER CHICKS!! YOU'RE NEVER BROKE!!" he cheerfully bellowed. *'Ahhh, he blew it.'* Blushing and retrieving her cell, she researched and dialed the BPD's non-emergency phone number. [Ring, Ring], "Berkeley Police Department. This is Regina. How may I assist you?" she asked.

"Good Afternoon, this is Detective Harriet Wilburn from the Southern Crest Police Department......" As she continued, from a distant, she recognized a familiar face. Immediately, she enthusiastically waved at her younger sister, who was styling a curly, sandy blonde ponytail; wearing a black gym suit, with a white tank top; along with a modest gold necklace and digital wristwatch. Upon approach, they warmly greeted each other. Standing directly in front of *'Far Out,'* Carol fancifully swirled around, and eagerly pointed at an official 11x14, white piece of paper that was taped on the double glass door. In big bold letters, it read, *"UNDER CONSTRUCTION."*

"Look! I told you. Isn't that great?" she hinted. "No, it's not. I really wanted to see Mister Man as well. I called him late last night, but he must have changed his cell number, and no one answered at his shop," she disappointedly replied. Taking a deep breath, "What's another nearby alternative? Preferably one where they sell booze."

Chapter 3

<u>Monkeying Around</u>

Pointing up the street, "I know, let's go to 765's," Carol suggested. "I'm not trying to be inconsiderate, but I don't want to have coffee at some ritzy joint. Where the price for an ordinary glazed donut is the same as a gallon of gas. And what's up with the numbers? 765's? Why don't café owners select traditional names such as George's, Tony's, or Ben's?" she griped. "You'll like it. They expanded their patio area and added new fall colored chairs; along with extra wide tables, big umbrellas, and overhead heaters if it gets cool. It's well-designed.

It's also the absolute spot to sip and chat without any major interruptions," she persuasively said. "Lead the way." Once they entered, "What kind swanky place is this?" Harri intriguingly asked. "Every week, they feature a new food theme. Studying the interior, "This week, it appears they're highlighting desserts made with bananas," Carol replied. Peering through a refrigerated glass display, they marveled at the banana fritters, nut breads, signature cookies, puffs, cakes with cream cheese frosting, and many other delectable sweets.

To further entice their customers, they also set aside a display tray, which held several miniature cups of banana pudding with vanilla wafers. Since Harri has a sweet tooth, she readily sampled a lavish helping, "Um, um, this is heavenly, and it's going straight to my love handles," she garbled.

Snatching a yellow cap from a nearby rack, and plopping it onto her head, "You know what that makes you?" Carol jokingly asked. "Yea, I get it." Swiftly, she placed her cup on top of the counter, and impersonated a lively ape. Then, she crazily sprung over and playfully scratched her sister's tummy. Hysterically laughing and tapping her head, "Alright, Bonzo, just because you're the Banana Police, doesn't give you the authority to tickle women." Continuing with their hilarity, "Then, let's slip out of here," she said with a giggle. Comically, bracing herself against the edge of the counter, "Only if you can manage to peel me away." Approaching the display, a male associate with a name tag that read, *Mark from Napa,* courteously asked, "Ladies, could I assist you with anything?" "A cage for two seems fitting," Harri quipped.

"We're fine. We're headed to the patio," Carol happily replied. Grinning from ear to ear, "You were both entertaining. I'm glad we have your performance on video. I'll show it to my co-workers at lunch time. I'll just have to fill in the audio portion," he said. "Oooh, you should send me a copy. Who wouldn't mind viewing a cop monkeying around?" Carol sunnily imagined. With a deadpan expression, "Oh brother, I can hear them back at the station. Hey, let's watch Harri act like a zany chimpanzee for the 216th time!" she grumbled. "You're making too much of this. You'll be giving your co-workers a delightful treat. They'll get a big kick out of it."

Without hesitation, she removed the floppy hat and retrieved her wallet. "Mark, here's my business card. Undoubtedly, my intentions were to entertain my silly sister, not social media.

So I would really appreciate you not posting our satire." "Yes, ma'am. No worries," he kindly uttered. Strolling away, "Gosh that pudding was incredibly rich. I'll be tipping the scale tonight. Remind me again, why you chose this place?" she asked. "Never mind girlie, follow me. The patio is over there," she answered while pointing in its general direction. Upon entry, the glorious sun was breaking through the gray cloudy skies, and it seemed to be awaiting their very arrival. Scanning over the area, they settled on a pale orange, round patio table, with four cushy chairs, along with a matching umbrella. Removing her jacket and scarf, Harri intentionally sat with her back against the boxwood hedges, which provided an unobstructed view of the entry.

Peering around, "No one has come to take our order. What's going on?" she whined. Promptly, she stood up, "Let me find someone who actually works here." Preoccupied with her cell phone, Carol transitorily looked up, and pointed to the umbrella pole, "Sorry. I should've told you. See the brown latch on the side?" she asked. "Yep." "Slide it open, scroll downward, and you'll see their menu. Be a dear, and order me an *English Breakfast,* and four banana fritters. Bonnie texted me something or other..." she murmured. As requested, she submitted their order, and a receipt instantly appeared on her cell phone. "How's the j-o-b?" she inquired.

"Usually, it's hectic during the summer and every holiday season. However, for some reason, we've been swamped all year." Faintly, rubbing the back of her neck, "That's good, isn't it?" "Yes, sort of. Currently, we only have a handful of physical therapists on staff.

Recently, we've successfully developed a tight-knitted community within our clinic. So we're continuously booked." "In other words, you guys have been turning away new business." "Um hum, precisely. Though, the majority of our patients prefer our in-house services, lately, we've been recommending some self-help techniques, such as enrolling into a fully equipped fitness gym." "How's the moola?" she asked. Nodding in disbelief, "After I passed probation," she partially conveyed. "How long is that?" "Ninety days." "I received a measly thirty cent raise." "EEK." "I know. When I was close to my annual, the company arbitrarily announced, no wage increases across the board," she disappointedly conveyed. "What's making you stay?" she asked.

All of the sudden, a young male server entered the patio area. Noticeably, underneath his white apron, he was wearing a black tee-shirt and jeans, which were also drooping in the rear; two tin-foil caps, with the brims slightly facing opposing directions; and an expensive pair of matching tennis shoes that were intermittently flashing gold lights. Caught off guard, "Is it New Year's already?" Harri wisecracked. "That's Aaron." Placing their order on the table, "I know Miss Carol loves anything made with sugar. So the banana fritter is hers," he said. "Oooh yummy," she remarked as she retrieved her fork. "But which one of you ladies ordered the tea?" "Dude, do I remotely look like a tea teetotaler?" Harri smugly asked.

Shifting his slender torso, "*Excusez – Moi* ("excuse me"). Ma'am, are you aware that a teetotaler has virtually nothing to do with sipping steamed tea leaves?"

Minimally, repositioning his hats, "In all candor, you look like you wouldn't blink, if I accidentally slipped you a double shot," he impolitely teased. [A hip hop's ring tone rang], "Is that your cell?" Harri questioned. "Nope." Speedily, retrieving his cell from his rear pants pocket, "What's up P dog? No, uh, it's you, bro!" he animatedly yammered. Without warning, he dropped off a few napkins, and strutted away. "How (expletive) rude! What a smart aleck!" "Don't unsnap your girdle," Carol teased. Pointing at his backside, "No tip for you, buster!" Lifting her tea cup, "He doesn't need it. His parents own this place and eight others. Whenever they retire, it'll all be his." "And they have his wacky (expletive) waiting on tables?" she shockingly asked. "It's their earnest attempt to inject some humility into his consciousness. Overall, I give his parents an A for effort."

Setting down her coffee cup, "Before the dynamic host of 'Thursday Night Live' drops by again, you were telling me about your job," she said. "My problem is I have a college degree, but I'm limited on practical experience. I suppose I'll have to pay my dues like everyone says. In any case, I know our patients value my work. In our department, we're consistently rehabilitating those who are recovering from serious injuries such as back, carpal tunnel, hip, and knee surgeries."

"Speaking of which, before I return, could you hook me up? I have tension running all along my neck and shoulder areas, as well as my lower back." "Sure." "Any drama? You left that out," she cheekily encouraged. Raising one eyebrow, "Who's doing who?" she asked with a chuckle.

"That should've been your opening line." "Hum, none of the employees that I'm aware of are dating each other. HA! I have one right up your alley," she eagerly replied. "But you didn't hear it from me." "C'mon, I don't work at your company, never met your manager, or any of your co-workers, and I don't have the hotline number to the Enquirer." "Okay-okay-okay." "For some time, I was leery of a tall, thin, male patient, who consistently arrived wearing skimpy tight shorts, and a cut off tank top. Although, he wasn't my patient, I decided to snoop, and reviewed his chart. Accordingly, he had carpal tunnel surgery. What was interesting is he also had a habit of frequenting the men's restroom," she gullibly stated.

"What in the hell does that mean? Maybe the poor schmuck has a crummy prostate." Leaning forward, Carol whispered, "That's not it. I have it on good authority that he was a male prostitute." "Is he still going there for treatment?" she inquired. "Nope. For some unexplained reason, he simply disappeared, and I never found out why," she answered. "Not enough tricks. So he became miraculous healed." Pausing for a moment, "Hum, we're also occasionally visited by some eccentric homeless people." "Who isn't?"

"Bob, our clinics manager, is thought to be a modern day Romeo." "Now you're getting warmer," Harri chirped. Shaking her index finger, "Oooh on Valentine's Day, the receptionist reported that we were received a bounty of calls." "I'm assuming they were checking to see if you were open." "Nope." Widely grinning, "They were for Bob? Oooh, he must be a rocket in the sack," she excitedly presumed.

Rolling her eyes, "Yes, the calls were for him, but I don't have the slightest clue if he's an expert launcher. Getting back to my point, he was scheduled to be off that week. Midmorning, five or six women, I forgot exactly how many showed up. Anyway, they inquired of his whereabouts. Particularly, one distraught woman carrying an infant, kept coming in and out, until 11:00 o'clock. Before she left, she screamed at our nice receptionist, '...*you're probably in on it!*' Then, she threatened to kick his you know what." "You still don't swear?" Harri asked. "Only if I'm highly provoked," she replied.

Waving her right hand, "Go on." "Later that afternoon, we were visited by a singing telegram." "What song did he perform?" "The messenger was a SHE! Her name was Choon Hee, and she sang, *'You ain't nothing but a hound dog,'*" she answered with a riotous laugh. "Was she dressed like Elvis?" she interestingly asked. "Yesss!" she howled. Dabbing her eyes, "Harri, she wore an outlandish pompadour black wig, and a white and gold sequin, skin tight jumpsuit that possessed a gigantic collar. She was brilliant! I was so mesmerized by her impersonation that I plum forgot to record it. When she first arrived, they told her that Bob was on vacation.

Then, she said, *'It's paid for ladies. Time to rock n' roll!'* In no time flat, she switched on her karaoke machine, grabbed the microphone, shimmied and shook her tiny hiney, and tore up the lobby floor. Before we knew it, a sizeable crowd formed, and everyone clapped along. She instantly turned into a rock star! Altogether, she received fifty eight dollars in tips." "Not bad for three to four minutes of work," she quipped.

"Don't forget the encore. The following week, when he returned, the guys coined a waggish nickname for him." "Bow Wow?" she predicted. "No, it's Biggy Bob," she responded with a giggle. "No offense, Carol, but your job is so borrrring. I mean, I can't believe no one hasn't ever kicked the (expletives) from underneath someone's crutches," she said. "We don't promote violence." "We don't either. But every once in a while, to keep us on our toes, you'll find one of us placing the other in a headlock," she said with a chuckle. "Where did you get such a sinister mind?" "I was an abandoned child." "Do tell," she amusingly asked.

"Is the San Francisco office your only location?" "No, we have four others around the East Bay." "Perhaps the elevator music makes up for the company's shortcoming," she funnily hinted. "Hardly. However, I must admit I enjoy working with the patients, and I'm trying to remain mindful that we're not supposed to be exclusively enriching our lives. We're also should be assisting others as well. So I'll stay until I feel it's time." "How's your boss?" Harri asked. "You're thinking of Veronica. She was terminated six months ago for cursing at a disabled patient whose insurance carrier was slow in paying. Abe is presently our new manager," she replied. "Woo, is he married?" "Happily, and he has four children. So forget him." "Did she find another job?" "I believe so. Janis, one of my co-workers, told me that she's working at a local casino." "As?"

Shrugging her shoulders, "Don't know." "Maybe she's a hat check girl," she readily joked. "Does those jobs even exist?" "Call Mom, she's an authority on everything," she mockingly responded.

"You need to stop. Anyway, she was the worse." "Don't ever say that." "Why?" "You're jinxing yourself." "Think so?" "Several years ago, I said the same thing to Brock concerning our previous Lieutenant. Unbelievably, the next one was ten times as worse." "Is that even humanly possible?" Carol asked. "Have you ever watched "Special Report," on the 11 o'clock news?" "Was he or she a screamer?" "Yes and no. He was an alcoholic," she dryly replied. "Oh my. Whenever I've had the misfortune of working for someone like that, it makes me seriously doubt the sensibilities of the hiring manager." "So Abe is cool?"

"He's a breath of fresh air, very personable, a big picture sort of supervisor. Within a short period, we've gone from a cold and sterile environment to a more caring one, whereas patients are sharing their past medical hardships as well as their stories of recovery. Overall, I believe they've finally grasp the concept that we should psychologically support one another. It's really refreshing to witness the fruits of our labor. We refer to it as, 'Peer Support,' she answered. "I'm glad you feel that you're contributing to others."

"Truthfully, I've never worked at a place that was recognized as life altering." "Then, I should inform you of another transformational environment." "Church," she hinted. "Such a noble response," she murmured. "I'm speaking of jail, girlfriend." "I was thinking in terms of something healthier." "For some folks, it is." "Touché." "Enough shop talk. How's my talented niece?" Harri asked. Scratching her outer ear, "I'm quite peeved with Bonnie. This year, she has been going through some kind of senseless, cultural, identity crisis," she tiresomely replied. "What's that about?"

"For starters, I'm Caucasian married to an African American, and unfortunately, Bonnie is a purist." Fingering the table from left to right, "It's either black or white, this or that, she has no faith in the gray," she answered. "In her mind, she's being helplessly squished by both worlds." "Exactly. The other morning, I called her to come downstairs, in order to help me with bringing in some supplies, and she irately shouted, *'Mom, I told you. That's not my name!'* "When did that start?" "I don't know. Everything is a blur. Three months ago, she came home from school with dreadlocks, and refused to wash her hair.

One day, while I was preparing dinner, she rushed downstairs and went into a tizzy, *'Why didn't you married someone within your own race? You and Dad never imagined me or Mason, or what kind of life we were going to have, did you? Mom, Mason isn't exactly happy either. Haven't you ever wonder why he seems like he doesn't know what he's doing? We don't perfectly fit in with the whites, blacks, or any other ethnic group for that matter. And where in the hell did you get my name? It's so (expletive) weak! From now on, call me Sierra! It's fresh, and it doesn't make me feel like I'm from a (expletives) Zebra Colony!'*

"Then, she stormed upstairs and slammed her bedroom door," she explained. "Did the hinges fall off?" she quipped. "Harri, it's not funny. Immediately, I started screaming at her to stop swearing, but I'm certain she was tuning me out." "How old is she?" "The ripe old age of fourteen." "She'll grow out of it," she assuredly advised. "It better happen soon." Simulating slashing her own throat, "Because I've had it up to here with her rhetoric.

To add insult to injury, she also announced that she's joining a political movement." "Which one?" Looking cross-eyed, "She hasn't decided yet. Now I'm overly concerned about her safety." "Whenever you find out, let me know, and I'll look into it." "These days, living with her is like having a non-stop throbbing toothache. No matter how much medicine is applied, it won't lessen," she irksomely stated. "When did she start swearing? And what did Eugene say?" "She obtained her disrespectful potty-mouth, around the same time you did," she sorely replied.

"That young." "Um hum, and she's worsening by the day. I usually don't say anything, because it'll only complicate matters. In regards to bubblehead, I've been waiting for his response. Since he refers to everyone as *'baby,'* similar to a Vegas entertainer, he doesn't want to be bothered with what he calls, *'trivial domestic issues.'* If I told him straight out that she's experiencing a major crisis, he'll run into her bedroom, have a short and sweet talk, line her pockets, kiss her on the forehead, and determine that I'm overreacting."

Chapter 4

Woo, Woo, Girl Talk!

Lowering her head, "I suppose this is the best time than any," Carol mumbled. "You're pregnant?" Harri asked. "Bite your tongue! For the better part of this year, Eugene has missed numerous important dates such as my birthday, our anniversary, Christmas Eve, and he used the same feeble excuse – *'meeting with a client.'* Then, last month, he came home after four in the morning. After I returned from work, I went through his clothes, and discovered two heart wrenching photos.

One was of a Polynesian woman wearing a one piece bathing suit. She was grinning while holding her stomach. The second one was a baby's ultrasound with the name of Gina Nguyen printed on the top left hand corner. They were both tucked inside his overcoat," she despondently shared. "Oh no, what a nightmare. He's clowning up a storm." "Clowning?" "He fits the description. The only thing missing from his two bit act are the giant, floppy, exploding shoes and the big red nose. Whew! The (expletive) bum got her pregnant!" she disturbingly stated.

"Um hum." "Have you confronted him?" "No." "Are you?" "What's the use? The mere thought of adding an innocent baby into this fiasco is more than enough." "If it was me, I would've jacked up his (expletives). At a minimum, give him something to remember me by," Harri spitefully stated. "Part of me would like to, but I don't want to quarrel anymore."

"What the (expletive)? He's so full of ^*&%@#! All this time, I thought you two were tighter than a drum. Although, you have to admit he does come across as the type who would sniff around. What's all the soft peddling about? Why haven't you kicked his (expletives) to the curb?" she quizzed. "My lawyer advised me to wait until he receives his next promotion, which will be coming up soon. Then, possibly, I'll file for a legal separation," she answered. "Isn't being in love incredibly childish?" "Now you're starting to sound like me," Harri gently teased.

"I'm serious. You meet some guy, a virtual stranger, who you unwisely proclaim to be your true love. What a joke! Then, down the road, you're so glad to be rid of him, that you'll happily swap him for a hideous pair of salt and pepper shakers from the 99 Cent Store. Heaven help me, what I'm about to say." "Do it," she urged. "Realistically, since it appears the vast majority are prone to cheating, I was pondering over the idea of termed marriages. One could choose a five or ten year plan, or it'll could automatically end on a selected date. What do you think?"

"In some ways, you're describing a prenuptial agreement. Currently, there are no term dates available, but the details are craftily spelled out. Don't discount your concept, term limits could be the future," she replied. "Scripturally, I'm aware we suppose to marry for life, but these days only a miniscule wants to fully cooperate. Picture playing basketball, where very few players are adhering to the rules," she clarified. "Have you considered what would happen to the children of the marriage?" "Obviously, I haven't thought this through.

I'm shooting from the hip." "That's where your idea falls short," Harri determined. "In the past, other far-fetched notions such as legalizing alcohol, marijuana, interracial and same sex marriages were once considered taboo. Who knows? Every day, more unimaginable things are becoming acceptable." "I truly believe in freedom of choice, but it makes me wonder when and where do we draw the line?" Carol theoretically questioned. "When did your relationship start falling apart?" "It's been on the decline for some time, but we kept up appearances until Mason left for college. That's when I started looking for a part-time job, and stopped behaving like Eugene's official door mat. We also no longer share a bed. And I know how he met her.

Early spring, I sent him on an errand – to a home improvement store, in order to repair our backyard fence. Guess whose name was listed as the sales clerk?" "What a (expletives)!" she wildly responded. "Don't you love paper receipts?" "Besides her name, what else do you know about her?" "Two weeks ago, I had to see her for myself. So Bonnie and I went there under the pretense of shopping for a new dishwasher. More or less, she's young, attractive, and the oversized smock was a dead giveaway. Before we left, Bonnie told her, *'Good luck. I hope it's a girl.'* "Oh gosh."

"Think in terms of salt being poured over an open wound. When we returned home, I reviewed a few social media websites, and found several photos of them. They looked like they were dating in San Francisco and Marin. Eugene thinks he's slick. He was overly confident that I would never visit such sites, and I rarely venture out to the city.

At her young age, I figured she would take some photos and post them. Under one caption, she wrote, 'The Love of My Life.' Snappishly, flipping her right hand, "Foolish child. On a lighter note, Bonnie and I admired her custom nails. They change colors depending on your body's temperature. Darn, I should've inquired where she goes," she half-jokingly said. Raising her eyebrows, "Bonnie doesn't know, right?" "No, but I can't wait to see his little colored girl's face when he breaks the news to her, because I'm not," she flatly replied.

"Colored?" "That's more of his nonsense. Some term of endearment – 'my little colored girl.' Every time he uses that colloquialism, it makes me want to vomit. I mean, who am I? His limp pancake batter? Oooh, he gets on my last nerve," she aggravatingly stated. "So he met Miss Thang in June?" Harri inquired. "According to the receipt, it was the day after Easter." "Old crook." "How do you think I feel?" "You sent hammer head on an errand, he picked up another woman, then the *@$%#%* gets her pregnant. Whew! What a lucky scumbag," she disparagingly remarked.

"Why?" "Because he's married to you. If he was married to me, our story would be featured on the six o'clock news." "At least we tried our best to properly raise our kids. Sometimes they're a challenge, but I suppose they're average. I know it's going to take some time to get over this colossal mess. In the morning, while I'm practicing yoga, I've been meditating over this matter. Recently, I've concluded that he'll be much happier without us.

Huh! Enough about me. How's Nathan? And how's my suave brother in law, Riggs?" Carol asked. "Hold onto your seat. First, your immature nephew called me this morning, and laid some heavy news on me," she hesitantly replied. "It seems he knocked up Linda, his selective amnesia girlfriend." "Nate is going to become a father?" "Yes, and I'm not too thrilled about it. During our conversation, I also unfairly criticized her." "You don't like her?" she presumed. Appearing as if she bit into something sour, "Fundamentally, what's not to like? She's sweet, young, and genuinely fond of my son.

Regrettably though, they're both riding in an unseaworthy vessel, with no life jackets. Neither one have faced any real hardships. Generally, I need a clearer picture of her true character, before I can say that she's right for him," she answered. "I understand. They're too naïve. In their youthful eyes, everything is an adventure." "You hit the nail on the head. Though, it didn't seem like he took my criticism to heart." Displaying a crooked smile, "I shouldn't have responded in such a discouraging manner," she regretfully conveyed.

"Don't beat yourself up. You were taken by surprised." "For the most part, I want Nate to have a chance to graduate from college, travel abroad, date career driven, independent thinking women, who also have goals and aspirations, and then, make a life-long determination based on experience, not purely because they attended the same high school. Call me a hypocrite, but that's what I want for him," she explained. "Nevertheless, in this tale of woe, there's one silver lining.

Recently, he finished a Fiber Optics certificate program, and landed a job. Clearly, he also needs to start saving more money." With a straightforward expression, "I might as well throw this in. Seven weeks ago, Riggs and I mutually called it quits. He's renting a studio nearby." Displaying a startling expression, "Oh no, what happened?" she asked. "Our work schedules never meshed. For the past two years, he has been working graveyards as a Watch Commander, and of course, I'm still working days. To sum it up, we haven't spent any quality time with each other, and he has become too self-centered. He also believed a date night every other month should suffice," she said.

"I'm so sorry. Though, I thought something was wrong. You look fabulous, but appear somewhat fatigued. How are you holding up?" "Most of the time, I feel exhausted. I can't seem to get a good night sleep – three to four hours tops. I guess I have insomnia." "It's no wonder. You're separated, work long hours, and you're under a tremendous strain. Why don't you take a leave of absence?" she asked. "No. Work is the cure. Staying busy, keeps the stress to a bare minimum." "You know what's best." "I know I made the right decision. I'm tired of keeping my head buried. And whenever we did go out, our big fun was so predictable and limited. I've also arrived at the conclusion that he only married me, because I became pregnant with Nate. As far as I'm concerned, I don't deserve a marriage for pity sake," she scornfully stated.

"Uh-uh. Don't go there. I remember when you guys started dating. I was a senior in high school. Everyone could see that Riggs was madly in love with you, and I envied you so much.

Sometimes I would dream that a fella like him, would feel the same way about me," she admitted. "You had a crush." "I guess I did. When you initially introduced him, his enormous built scared the heck out of me. But after he visited us a few times, I realized he was merely a sweet teddy bear. Remember, on Sunday afternoons, when we would all go swimming?" she giddily asked. With no response given, she continued, "I bet he's still a good swimmer. In those days, he had the most hilarious way of expressing himself. I know Mom and Dad also enjoyed his company. Indeed, you two were made for each other."

Swiping her bangs, "Yea, happy days. Carol, don't make me doubt myself," she unpleasantly mumbled. "Sorry." "In any case, your childhood hero has a lot to learn about keeping the romance alive. After our split, I immediately joined one of those popular dating websites, and met a bunch of uninspiring rejects. Four weeks ago, I enrolled into an unknown website, and met another set of prospects," Harri explained. Opening her purse, "Oooh, I should jot down the name of that second site." Speedily, placing her left hand over the clasp, "Not so fast." "You gave me the impression that the latter was superior to the former." "Only if you're part of the criminally insane," she joked. "What are you saying?"

"I'll first start off with Thomas 'Juicy Lips' Gilroy," she replied. "Ooh, he must have been a good kisser." "Heck if I know. His lips were so moist and wet, I kept imagining being kissed by a roaring car wash." "You wouldn't survive," she said, laughing.

"You think? He also flipped out a mini accordion and showed me pictures of his ten children." "Ten?" "Yep! Ten crumb snatchers. However, three were teenagers." "From the same mom?" she inquired. "Nope." "How many?" "Seven." "Did he marry any of them?" "Nope." "He's a double-crossing scoundrel." "Yep." Gesturing with her index finger, "Or maybe he needed a sizeable write-off," Carol jested. "Not nearly clever enough. Towards the end, the waitress brought the check. We had two coffees, and went halves on a slice of Bundt cake. The bill was $14.62 and he said, *'We'll split it.'* "Did you?" "No. Then, I told him, *'I'll take care of it.'*

Immediately, I moseyed up to the front counter, paid it, tipped the waitress, and left. Old cheapskate." she sordidly answered. "What did you expect? He's a shabby broken down man." "You don't have to convince me. The second one was Besnik *'Secret Agent'* Galica. His actual nickname is Lefty. That dude wasn't main stream at all. He had such a rough Albanian accent, it felt as if we were chatting while speeding in a (expletive) race car. I didn't understand much, but I laughed whenever he did. One thing I liked about him, he had an impressive shiner on his left hand. Admiring his swollen purplish knuckles was the highlight of my evening. I really dig strong men. However, once I zeroed in on him, something didn't sit well," she said. "What was it?"

"He had a distinct manner of speaking. Galica also reminded me of a ruthless drug dealer we arrested some time ago. At the time, I was a blonde, and he went by another name." "Are you sure?" she uneasily inquired. "Think so. To be on the safe side, I unchecked my availability status." "Smart."

"The third one was Kurt *'Beach Boo-Boo'* Garrison. Originally, we met for a few minutes at Biscuit's Dog Park. At the time, he was accompanied by his German shepherd, I forgot her name, and I had Grady, along with two of his companions. Luckily, his dog was a female, so Grady behaved. Anyway, when he approached, everything about him, screamed, *'Here's your beach playmate, baby!'* His sculptured face, shiny blonde hair, hazel eyes, and especially, his lean but muscular built, indicated plenty of fun in the sun, with that guy." "Oooh, I'm excited. Why won't you give me the name of the dating site?" she whined. "Give me a minute." "Alright, but make it snappy."

"After our brief introduction, we both returned home and checked our availability for an official date." "What did you wear?" she eagerly asked. "I didn't want to overplay my hand, so I wore a pair of blue jeans and my cream colored cashmere sweater, which happens to accentuate one of my best features." "Your knockers," she said with a snicker. "Um hum." "Where did you meet?" "Patience. I'll get to that." "Prior to our date, I found myself daydreaming about spending days on end with him at the beach. I vividly imagined Kurt wearing a pair of tight hugging, swimming trunks. And of course, I would be styling in my divine straw hat, and fetching turquoise swimsuit. You know, the one that has a dainty skirt that fastens on the side."

"You'll look stunning," Carol chimed in. "In addition, I would also bring a cooler filled with bottled waters, juices, and assorted cut fruit in a Tupperware bowl; along with my old transistor radio just for fun." "Sounds enchanting."

"Um hum. While lying on our brightly colored beach towels, we would be lightly chatting, occasionally stealing some tender kisses, taking a few dips, as well as rubbing oil on each other. Ahhh," she blissfully expressed. "Okay, I'm there. So what happened?" Carol impatiently asked. "We met at Barney's Taverns for cocktails, and he brought his dog." "Huh?" "It's his service dog," she blankly responded. "Oh my goodness." "There's more. The dog happened to stare up at me, so naturally I gently stroked her, and he rudely said, *'Don't pet her. She's working.'* "No way." "While seated at the bar, he said, *'I need to share something important with you.'* "What was it?" "He's bisexual." "Good golly, now I'm visualizing you with his male friend, lying in between the two of you."

"Me too! Oooh yuck! He also asked if that was going to be a problem." "And?" "I lied." "I know you did girlfriend," she remarked with a chuckle. "Afterwards, I kept looking for a large window." "Why?" "To throw my (expletives) out of it!" she dramatically answered. Gripping her coffee cup, "Shall I go on?" "Sure. This is entertaining, and I thought my life was uneventful." "The fourth one was Sean *'Slimy Sexpot'* McIntosh. Initially, I kinda liked him. He was soft spoken and easy on the eyes.

He previously owned a pawn shop in the San Fernando Valley. When I asked what he's currently doing, he was ambiguous. On our first official date, um, I ought to clean this up for you. We met for dinner at Pauley's, an Italian restaurant. Besides a conspicuous white circle surrounding his ring finger, and drinking me under the table, he was also engaging with his ping pong. If you get my drift," she said.

"You're kidding? You mean he was playing with you-know-what?" Puckering her lips and chuckling, "Shhh. Originally, I thought the schmuck dropped a spicy meatball in his lap. It wasn't too long before I realized what was going on." "What a pervert!" she exclaimed. "Somewhere in the midst of his cavorting, I couldn't stand looking at him anymore." "Weren't you upset?" Carol asked. "Nope, I've been too exposed. I'm so desensitized, if he had stripped, I would've probably applauded, and that's only if he impressed the hell out of me," she joked. "You should've arrested him." "I thought about it, but I wanted to finish eating my cannoli. They make the best." "How embarrassing." "Not for him. He was having a swell time underneath that red and white checker table cloth."

"What happened afterwards?" she asked. Squarely eyeballing her, "Oooh, you would've been proud of me. Instead of pinning his notorious (expletive) against the wall, I was very lady like, in supplying the standard," she humorously replied. Bobbing her head, "You had a headache." "Um hum. The next day, I conducted a thorough background check, and discovered he had a prior conviction of sexual assault. The way he was acting, I wasn't a bit surprise." "What prevented you from conducting a search, before going out with him?" she reasonably enquired.

"I didn't have ample time. This is what happened. While I was at home, I rushed through a bunch of profiles. Suddenly, I ran across his. Without thinking, I found myself approving for a *'meet and greet.'* Initially, we met at the park for ten minutes.

Once I arrived home, he sent a second request for dinner, and I foolishly confirmed within the hour. Two days later, when I returned to the office, that's when I discovered the ugly truth." "Is he a registered sex offender?" she asked. "Yep. So I contacted the dating website, and they knocked his obnoxious (expletive) off." With a sly gaze, "They're also refunding all of my fees, plus they're allowing me to continue searching." Fanning her face, "EW! He sounds icky! Let's not talk about him anymore. So far, you've been on four dates, and none of them were salvageable. How disappointing."

"Hold up, there's three more." "Tell it like it is, sis." "Then, number five was Roy 'Baggy Eyes' Bowen. Initially, he came across as a good old fashioned guy. On our second meet, he kissed me on the cheek, and I smelled some old, stale, crappy beer. That should've given me a heads up. Since I can also be a lush at times, I overlooked it. Though, the cop in me, wanted to remove the breathalyzer from my truck, but I didn't want to spoil the evening," she said. Slapping her thighs and laughing, "Girl, he also had the baggiest bags ever." "They were that big?" "Any droopier, and they could've carried our take out," she responded while she stretched her under eye skin.

"Oh brother, and his parents really missed the mark. They should've named him Beauregard. His sluggish manner of speaking reminded me of a Country Fried Steak. You don't mind having it as a meal once in a while. But you don't want to make a steady diet of it," she answered. "Is he from the South?" she asked. "Somewhere east of Sacramento. It's all the same."

Chapter 5

Chancy Prospect #7

"Then, number six was Mack *'Flaky Fool'* Madsen. He has a defined built, medium height, and a snow white buzz cut," Harri accurately described. "You certainly go for men with great bodies." "Who doesn't?" "I guess if it's available, why not?" Carol quipped. "In short, he has been divorced six times." "What was his longest stint?" "A year and a half, and he admitted that he was hanging by a thread after three months." "Incredible." "From what I gathered, he seems enthralled with the notion of planning and participating in the pre-marital festivities such as the rehearsal, bachelor's party, as well as the wedding ceremony and honeymoon." "But he's not too overjoyed with the prospects of dedicating several years of hard work associated with having a successful marriage," Carol presumed.

"Um hum. Once the honeymoon phases out, he does too. He sounded like someone who's continually searching for a psychological and/or physical high." "You're very perceptive." "That's a Police Officer's first line of defense." "So why did he join the dating site? What's he looking for? A companion, another wife, or a good friend." "I recommend a gerbil," she flatly replied. "Well, we don't have to wonder, who the culprit was, behind those failed marriages. You think he's bipolar?" she suggestively asked. "I'll wager a month's salary. He also accused his third wife of blowing up his Cadillac, another lucky devil," she answered as she graphically demonstrated with both hands. "Lucky?" "He wasn't in it." "Did he file a Police report?"

Shaking her right index finger, "Uh-uh. Right there, I said to myself, he's full of trouble." "Geez, another one down the tubes." "Um hum. During our brief time together, I was checking him out. The way he kept looking over his shoulders, as if he was anticipating a lousy tap. I believe Mack is also a hardcore gambler. The more likely version of someone destroying his vehicle is this. He probably owed a loan shark some big bucks. Since he failed to make good on his bet, the bookie probably sent over his henchmen to even the score. So they poured some gasoline all over his vehicle, stuffed some rags underneath it, lit a match, and a minute later - Wham! That's a clear message." Setting down her tea cup, "I should say so," she remarked. Wincing a bit, "Oooh, I almost forgot, he took a bus to our date," she said with a frown. "A bus? Did you see him get off?"

"No, but when he sat down, he sneakily slid a transfer inside his jacket pocket. At the time, he was rapping hard, while maintaining eye to eye contact - an old trick, but I caught it." "He knew he was out of his league." "More like out of his mind," she quipped. "You were circling the drain with that character." "Yep." "What a poor first impression. He should've at least hailed a cab." "Oh pleeeasse! Listen to this," she said with a disdainful gaze. "That bozo inquired whether the salted pretzels on our table were free." "What an idiot. Tell me, did he also wear a wide brim, full length fur coat, fake diamonds, and thick sole shoes?" Carol amusingly asked. "Now that would've been artful."

"Finally, last but not least, was Hammond Harris. He was number seven." "Wait, you forgot to attach a ridiculous nickname?" "He doesn't need one."

"Okay, I'll listen and figure out one." "Whatever. Well, as soon as I laid eyes on him, there was an instant attraction. This hunk of a man has deep sea blue eyes, straw-colored hair, tall, lean, with an impressive six pack; tight set of buns, and an oomph of a smile," she vividly described. "For kicks, I bet the school kids called him Hambone. Hey, that's it, Hambone," she said with a laugh. "But he does sounds dreamy." "Alright, Carol," she snapped. "His full name is Hammond Wilton Harris, but he goes by Wilt. However, you need to slow your roll. There's a snag." "How big?" she asked. "He works part-time as a male stripper at Leo's, which I can kind of look pass that." Glancing at the ceiling, "I knew he was too good to be true. So I purposely delayed running a thorough background check. Finally, last week, I discovered he has a record for felony burglary, and a misdemeanor assault," she related with a sigh. "Oh GOD."

"In 2013, he served sixteen months in Chino; court ordered to devote twelve hundred hours of community service; and spent a year and a half in anger management classes," she added. "Oooh, what I've always wanted. A great looking guy with a degree in Anger Management. How delightful," she cynically remarked. "I didn't know you were searching for a sparring partner? And burglary? Did anyone get hurt?" "No one was harmed. However, similar to most men, with the exception of Dad, Mister Man, and sometimes Brock, we could safely add him to the list of imbeciles. Before you conclude that I've totally lost my mind, let me make something perfectly clear, Wilt is under a limited engagement. So for the moment, I'm going to enjoy our harmonious arrangement."

"Duration?" "Um, three to six months should get rid of the cobwebs." "Six months??" she carelessly shouted. "I thought you were in the ballpark of a week or two. Have you gone cuckoo?" "C'mon, give me some credit. I said, I'm unsure." "Grant it." "For all I know, our affair could run its course within a few days. Hey, while I'm at it, I should also inform you of one disconcerting aspect that could make me call it quits." Laughing out loud, "Are you going to mix some lima beans with that Hambone? Get it?" Carol hilariously asked. "Why did I ever reveal his birth name?" she regretfully mumbled. Gesturing with her right hand, "Go ahead." "Despite his age, he's also into playing games." "I'm speechless. What kind?" she asked while nodding in disbelief.

"The other day, he mentioned his cell phone will soon be cut off, because he doesn't get paid until the following week," she replied. "And?" "And nothing, I could give a rat's (expletive) if he can't pay his bills. He's a grown man. I'm not his mother. When it comes time, I'm sure he'll miraculously find a way to keep it on." "How lame." "No argument there. Needless to say, the opposite sex are definitely some strange creatures. However, I suppose in an effort to get along, we're expected to digest some of their (expletives)." "And vice versa. Though, in his case, he reminds me of a trifling con man," Carol said.

"We'll see. I also ran a general background check on his immediate family. Practically all of them have spent some time behind bars, except their grandmother, on his mother's side. I'm assuming after listening to everyone else jailhouse adventures, she became disinterested in committing a serious crime, or maybe she has an aversion to wearing bright orange.

Get this, he has also hinted about us living together. Mind you, so far, he's the best out of seven," Harri shared. "The best?? He's a piece of crap! Heck, he probably has an ulterior motive?" "Like?" Shrugging her shoulders, "I don't know. I'm just rattling off possibilities. Men like Hambone..," she barely stated. "Carol, his name is Wilt." "Whatever. His kind gets under my skin." "Why?" "The way they freely bounce from pillar to post. One day, they're driving a late model sedan and owning a home, in a private upscale community. The next thing you know, their waiting for a tardy bus, couch surfing, and sponging off their elderly parent's; or their wet behind the ears girlfriend; and/or committing a crime. What's wrong with some men?" she aggravatingly asked.

"Many were improperly raised. So they don't have the faintest idea how to conduct themselves. Some spent too much time chasing women, rather than business opportunities. Others took too many uncalculated financial risks and suffered tremendous losses; and the rest have a poor understanding of life as a whole. Once Nate started working, we began schooling him on the importance of saving money. Two weeks ago, I checked on-line, and he has roughly eleven hundred dollars in his savings, and ninety four dollars in his checking account," she answered. "Money management is certainly a positive discussion to have with young people," Carol chimed in.

"Although, I've complained about his spending habits, he seems to be on track, especially for someone his age. He also knows that whatever he earns, we expect him to put at least ten percent away."

"I'm glad we're discussing this subject. When Mason calls next week, I'm going to reinforce that savings strategy. Boy, I hope he doesn't take after his father. If he does, he's doomed. Eugene makes a fairly decent salary, but he doesn't respect money. The other day, I gave him $250.00, which should've lasted for the week. When he returned home, he only had three dollars, and some change. That's ridiculous," she commented. "Don't forget Gina, his mistress. I suppose he's obliged to squander some bucks on her." "You're right, of course," she said with a disgraceful expression. "Carol, sorry, it's an occupational habit. I'm used to being direct." "It's okay. I need to face facts." "Generally, there's a bunch of wobbly dudes who's doesn't give a hoot about financial stability, until they find their selves in a (expletive) sling," Harri added.

"If I didn't manage our monthly budget, we would probably come home one day with the electricity shut off, and a dozen of past due pink slips hidden in the back of a barely used drawer. Hum, I was just thinking. You know what your dating escapades remind me of?" she asked. "Grade school." "They're analogous to frequenting a dented can store. Do you remember the one Mom used to drag us to, on the corner of University and San Pablo Avenue? People all around the bay, flocked to that very store. In its heyday, it was held as a shopper's paradise. Comparable to your half-baked dates, they might be considered the best in town," she said with a snicker.

"EEK." "Gotcha!" "Oh, now were playing tit for tat, eh?" Harri plainly asked. "Sorry, we seldom see each other. Let's keep examining your latest prospects. It's far more interesting.

Question - why did you stop at number seven? Personally, I would've kept going. You might have hit the jackpot with eight, twelve, or twenty for that matter." "It did cross my mind." "More than likely, Wilt can't even afford to pick up some of your favorite snacks," she skeptically commented. "Do you realize what we've been discussing?" Harri soberly asked. "Um hum." "Don't you feel that we've spent too much time in (expletive) loser land?" "Give me another option. Neither one of us wants to hop the fence." "Agreed." "The way I see it, available men are like shopping for ripe strawberries. Sometimes to assemble one decent basket, you have to inspect several. Without saying, it takes time to distinguish the good and fair, from the ruined ones." "Point taken. And I'll tell you this, I have no intentions of allowing whomever to become the handsome, but financially dependent boyfriend."

Waving her right hand, "Pleeeasse! I don't know why some women put up with such nonsense." Carol disturbingly stated. "A lazy (expletive) lying in my bed all day is out of the question," Harri added. "In Wilt's case, he's simply a fling. Think of him, as my midnight madness. And if he can't manage to occasionally buy some of my favs, then that's a definite deal breaker." "Seriously, do you believe you could continue seeing him without developing feelings?" she asked. "Watch me. The problem is you're still seeing me with the same, old, tired lenses you wore when we were kids. Presently, I'm more concerned with contributing to my 401k, than forking over some hard earned dough, in order to support a pitiful bench player. I figured we'll play our parts. Then, when the fat lady sings, and she will, it'll be time to move on.

If he needs a woman to be his, um, sponsor, he'll have to persuade some hopeless broad." Wide eyed, "And that's your plan for Hambone?" "Stop saying that! You're going to make me repeat that ridiculous nickname to his face." "I love it," Carol remarked. "Anyway, back to what I was saying, Riggs wasn't a perfect mate, but he was never a financial burden. From time to time, Nate runs a little lean, but he doesn't ask for much," she said. "When you mentioned Wilt relishes playing games, I was wondering, aren't all men guilty of that?" "Some more than others." "For the past year, every time Eugene and I speak to each other, it rapidly evolves into an argument. Two weeks ago, I was highly upset with him, because he promised to teach Bonnie how to drive on Saturday mornings.

When it was time for him to live up to his promise, he claimed that he had a hectic schedule, and the weasel left before she got up. Then, I was compelled to become fast and loose with the truth. Later, I took her myself. That evening, we bitterly quarreled, and I released some unchoice words. You know what he said?" she asked. "Hum." Mimicking Eugene's voice, *Carol, you're too (expletive) selfish!*' At the time, we were situated in the kitchen. I swear I had to force myself to move into the dining room, so I wouldn't smack the back of his thick skull with our toaster. That's one thing he has in common with your friend." "Playing games?" "Yes. He also suffers from memory lapses, whenever it's convenient." "By any chance, is he related to Linda, Nate's girlfriend?" she coolly inquired.

"Don't think so. For example, in the past, I'm the one who regularly managed all of the kid's extra curriculum activities, and he referred to me as selfish? What a con.

He must have adopted that mumble jumble when he was in his fraternity," she said. "Huh, or a gang. Let's move on. Unless, you want to hear more about Wilt's rockin body." "Is he seeing other women?" Carol asked. "No." "Harri, you should know that you're not the only woman who finds him attractive. He's probably dating others. Do you care?" With a somber expression, "Perhaps he was, but I'm certain that he stopped once we became involved." Refreshing her tea cup, "Don't be delusional, and don't force him to lie to you," she astutely advised. "Could we change the subject?" Leaning forward and staring directly into her eyes, "Wilt isn't even orbiting the same hemisphere as Riggs." "Um hum." "Okay, I'll move on. I know what I'm about to say is going to sound egocentric, but I'm going to say it anyway.

Prior to marrying Eugene, and even afterwards, I've met many men who seemed intelligent and savvy within their chosen field. Though, I have yet to run across a guy who is earthy, smart, humorous, and charming. Clearly, I failed at completing my homework, because I thought Eugene fit the mode. It wasn't until after we were married that I painfully discovered his biggest flaw is his inability to commit," she sadly professed. "Carol, I've discovered their major flaws were always apparent, we just chose to look the other way."

Lowering her head and fiddling with a paper napkin, "What a dirty little trick life has played on us. We're all futilely searching for true love, something that's scarcely obtainable." With her petite right hand inching towards her heart, "It's a cruel fairytale. The possibility doesn't even exist," Carol softly cried.

"Don't cry. I can't stand it." Swiftly, Harri scooted her chair closer, and they lovingly embraced. "Most of these men are nothing like our father. Overwhelmingly, the majority lack honesty, dignity and respect. Often times, it's like dating a wayward teenager. Honey, you didn't do anything wrong. Like many women, you fell for the old okey-doke. Trust me, someday the right guy will find you," she assuredly advised. Wiping her eyes and nose, *'Wishful thinking,'* she pessimistically thought. Thereafter, [*'Ring, Ring'*], peeking into her purse, "Not mines," Carol snapped.

Speedily, retrieving her cell and reviewing the number, "Hey baby, I'm sitting here with my sister (chuckling). Did you get my message? I left you one early this morning, saying that I was going to be in the Bay Area for a couple of days," Harri gleefully said. "That's right, too bad sugar. I was going to invite you to lunch," Wilt responded. "You're not rehearsing this afternoon?" "Not until 4:00." "When are you coming home?" he inquired. "Tomorrow evening." "You want me to swing by?" "If you want," she provocatively replied. "You've got yourself a date! And babe, wear that smokin red lingerie, you bought especially for me, panties optional," *['Click'].*

Blushing, giggling, and resting her cellphone on the table. "Was that Brock?" "Wilt," she self-consciously answered. "You're behaving like a dizzy adolescent, and if Granny were here, she would also add, that *'you're no spring chicken.'* With a peculiar grin, "From a twisted angle, it's doesn't seem too shady, does it?" she awkwardly asked.

"You've effectively performed a 180. Think about it, you're dating a male stripper, who's potentially supplementing his income by engaging in porn." "Hey, I'm strictly operating under a need to know basis," she arrogantly stated. "If you're exclusively seeing him, you can't wear blinders forever. Some time ago, I read an article that reported over 70% of convicted felons weren't able to secure full time employment. Take the long view, with his criminal record, what kind of future will he be able to scrape together? Certainly nothing substantial." "As usual, you're stretching everything way out of proportion. Anyway, he has paid his debt to society." "Um hum."

"Haven't you ever heard of giving someone a second chance?" Harri defensively asked. "As a Christian, I believe in giving several. However, I'm not a Police Officer, who swore to abide by a certain code of conduct and ethics." With a distrustful gaze, "Carol, I hope you're not going to tattletale." "Uh-uh. In this scenario, no official meddling is required. As the Bible teaches us, everything done in the dark, will ultimately come to light."

Chapter 6

"No Such Thing as Chaotic Peace"

"Did you inform any of your prospects that you're a cop?" Carol asked. "No, what's the point of making them feel intimidated or insecure? Presently, they all believe I'm a professional dog walker. Whenever I agree to meet, I'll commonly recommend Biscuit's Dog Park. Of course, Grady leads the charge," Harri answered with a grin. "You should be grateful that he can't squeal." "And knowing him, he would, if he could. Anyway, since Reggie, our next door neighbor, doesn't get home until late in the evening, I'll usually take Aries and Zephyr with us. Then, Presto-O Change-O, I'm a dog walker. Customarily, it's the second date when things veer south," she explained.

"In my opinion, the wisest thing you could to do is to put all of this foolishness behind you. You seem to be using your worse instincts. This is so unlike you," she disappointedly mentioned. "I recognize it." "I wasn't eavesdropping, but aren't you planning on seeing Hambone tomorrow?" "You're relentless. Yeah, so? He's 36, with a magazine's cover physique. Carol, he's all that and a bag of chips," she convincingly replied. "Gosh, I assumed he was age appropriate. You're almost ten years older. Hopefully, you haven't lost all of your senses, and invited him over." "Only four times."

Wildly eyed, "Did you remove your guns?" she astutely inquired. Retrieving her cell and keying in a reminder, "Oooh, I'm glad you mentioned that.

I better lock up my Beretta, 9mm Glock 26, and Winchester rifle." "Where are they?" "My service revolver (Beretta), is tucked between the mattress and box spring; Glock is in the kitchen; and my rifle is lying on the top shelf in my bedroom closet." "Geez! You really haven't thought this through," Carol remarked. "Oops, I almost forgot my 40 caliber. But that should be okay. It's stored in Grady's closet," she abruptly mentioned. "You're going to get into a heap of trouble, if your commanding officer finds out." "He won't." "I take it, Nate still lives at home." "Um hum." "Has he met Ham hock?" "You mean Hambone. Oh now, you've got me saying that," she said, laughing. "They've ran into each other twice. Both times were late at night. He was leaving and Wilt was arriving." "How did Nate react?"

"Wishy-washy. Could you stop grilling me, and get to the point?" "Give me a second. How old was Nate when you guys bought your home?" Staring outwardly, "He was in the first grade," she answered. "And he and Riggs are still close?" "Sure." "That's one aspect our parents had indisputably correct. If the earth is off its axle, and a bunch of mindless folks are eating lox and bagels, while literally standing on their heads, doesn't mean that we should necessarily be following them. Do you get my point?" With a bewildered gaze, "You have to know, I would never consciously hurt Nate. I'm just trying to find some peace and happiness."

"Dearie, I have news for you, there's no such thing as chaotic peace. You can have one or the other, but not both. In addition, keep in mind, he has only seen you in the company of his father, or one of your male partners.

Seeing a complete stranger, entering into your home, without advance warning is considered reckless, rude, and inappropriate. Similar to teenagers his age, he'll play it cool for a while, but your separation is undeniably affecting him," she stated. "Prior to Riggs leaving, we briefly spoke with him. However, I fell short. Um, you're right," she admitted. "I shudder the thought of you and Riggs not mending your fence. But if not, then you need to speak with Nate right away. Thoroughly explain how you're planning to proceed, and allow him amble time in getting accustomed to the idea that you'll be dating other men. For a while, you should meet your gentlemen callers outside of your home. I know I'm not the one who typically lends advice, but you need to act responsibly," she aptly recommended.

Resting her left hand against her forehead, "With so much going on, it's difficult staying centered." "Let me say this, and then, I'll put a lid on it. Our children are under our watch for only a fleeting moment. You and Nate have a good mother-son relationship. Don't hand him a valid reason to resent you." "I don't want that. Carol, I'm going to take your advice, but up to a point. There's no way in hell that I'm going to stop having male friends from visiting my home. I've worked extremely hard for it, and I plan to entertain whomever I want, whenever it suits me. You should also know I'm not afraid of defending myself. I've been in law enforcement for over fifteen years, and I didn't earn my stripes solely based on time served." "I know."

"I'm also highly trained to sense when something is about to go down, or if someone is lurking in the shadows," she assertively added.

"Well, I'm not in law enforcement..." "You've got that right." "Then, humor me. Based on what you've previously shared, the last time you were involved in a one-on-one with a dangerous and volatile suspect, you were on patrol. At the time, your partner was also heavily preoccupied, and that occurred several years ago. With Wilt, you're all alone with a felon, in the privacy of your home. If you continue seeing him, you're bound to disagree. Do you know what ticks him off?" "He says jealousy." "Does he possess violent tendencies?" "No." Opening a pack of sweetener, "Does he have the cooties?" "The cooties? How did you dig up that word?" "You forgot, I still have a teenager with pimples, who's living at home," she flatly replied.

"Are you're referring to a STD (Sexual Transmitted Disease)? Why didn't you just say that?" she irritatingly questioned. "Too formal." "To answer your inquiry, prior to becoming intimate, we showed each other our latest health report." "Did he supply you with a current one?" she doubtfully asked. "Yes. You're trying to cover every angle, aren't you?" "I guess so. Question - once you've ran through all of your sexual fancies, what's left?" she sensibly asked. "Well, we both enjoy working out at the gym, and we love Mexican food," she nonchalantly responded. "That's it? Two categories?" Displaying a startled expression, "Did the buzzer go off? I need more time!" she kiddingly protested. "You should've told me that we were going to be featured on a live quiz show. Which one is my camera?" she said as she swiveled her head and laughed. "You're in denial." Lifting her eyebrows, "Correction, I'm in lust."

"Joke all you want. But I believe you need to thoroughly examine your fly-by-night affair, and ask yourself - Is he really worth the risk? And your brilliant scheme of keeping him a secret could go up in smoke, at any time, especially, since you reside within SCPD's territory." "It won't," she snapped. "Forgive me for saying, but you sound misguided." "I sound that bad?" "Um hum. Are you lonely? Why don't you stay down here for a while?" she suggested. "No. I'll be a lot healthier once Riggs finish moving the rest of his things. It bothers me every time I know that he has been in the house.

Due to our work schedules, we should never run into each other, but when he drops by to pick up something, he consistently leaves a sign." "Remember, he's working long hours, and trying to move as well," she murmured. Sticking out her left boot, "Yea, yea, for instance, you probably can't tell that I'm wearing two different sizes, compliments of your egghead brother in law," she complained. "That's a cheap shot. Isn't it plausible that you could've mixed up your own boots? Girlie, I thought you stopped holding onto your old shoes ages ago. Donate those puppies." Staring at her foot ware, "Too bad their two different sizes. Otherwise, I would cart them off with our donation to the Salvation Army in San Francisco," she said.

"Good idea. When I get home, I'm going to gather all of my unwanted shoes, and give them to a local shelter. Nate also has some nice clothes and shoes that are in good shape, and he doesn't wear them anymore. That's a waste." "It'll certainly prove to be a blessing to someone in need. Why didn't you notice the disparity once you placed them on?" Carol enquired.

"I hardly had time to put on my makeup, let alone double check that my shoes were correctly paired. Furthermore, I shouldn't have to do that. To put it bluntly, Riggs is a (expletive) irritant. He has reverted to a naughty three year old. Besides switching my shoes, last week, I found an unfamiliar brand of toothpaste setting on the counter in the master bathroom. It's in a small can, and it's gritty as (expletive)." "A new brand?" she presumed. "Whatever it is, it taste ghastly, and smells like old musty wallpaper. Who in the hell have ever heard of toothpaste in a can?" she maddeningly questioned.

"What's the name?" 'Spotty,' something like that." "I never heard of it. But I also haven't had a chance to freely explore the internet, or watch television in a while. Evidently, we've missed their commercials. How do you use it? Just dip your brush?" she genuinely asked. "Scoop or dip, either way, it's disgusting." "Is it made by a well-known company?" Shrugging her shoulders, "Who knows?" Harri snapped. "Who bought it?" Rolling her eyes, "Let's do a process of elimination. Shall we?" she disdainfully suggested. "It wasn't Nate. He's too immature to care. And Grady has been previously scolded about going to the grocery store unaccompanied. So that leaves Riggs, and he knows I don't like trying anything new that hasn't been highly recommended.

Anyway, since I couldn't locate a regular tube, I tried it, and my teeth bonded together like (expletive) glue," she pathetically responded. "If you honestly suspect something isn't kosher, common sense dictates that you toss the revolting product in the trash." "No way, I need to catch him in the act.

So I plan to continue using it until I'm seriously ill, but not too close to death's door, where I can't call for help." In a puzzling tone, "Talking about Brock and Riggs, you're the one going nuts. I should contact Bellevue and reserve an extra-large padded room," she wearily said. "I admit that I'm sleep deprived, but I'm as sane as the next person." "And that's not saying much," she muttered. "Deep down, you know he's not trying to poison you. Clearly, the infamous toothpaste isn't toxic, because you're plainly sitting here talking to me." "It could be a slow acting formula. Carol, make sure to call me day after tomorrow, and see how I'm doing."

"If you're not going to trash it, and you're that paranoid, take it to your lab, and have it tested," she suggested. "Good idea." "When Mason was five, he swallowed some white kiddie's glue in kindergarten. Once the school notified me, I left work, frantically picked him up, and rushed to Children's Hospital. Twenty minutes later, the pediatrician advised, *'Based on the small amount he digested, there's a chance that he might develop a mild stomach ache, but I doubt it.'* "You're not being dismissive, are you?" she upsettingly questioned. "Not at all. I'm simply pointing out that you're not conclusive if Riggs is pulling a harmless prank. Since you're exhausted, you're also over analyzing everything. From what I've observed throughout the years, break ups are extremely difficult on everyone concerned, even if it's your own idea."

"Perhaps you're right. However, if I sniff one more practical joke, all bets are off, and I'll have a chat with his Lieutenant, if I survive," she weirdly stated.

"Make certain all of your ducks are in a row, before you file an official complaint. Riggs may have his priorities disorganized, but he has always been a principled man. Thankfully, he's not a two-faced slime ball, like Eugene." Swiftly, waving her right hand, "Let's go back to Wilt. If you ask me, no guy from a second-rate dating site is worth it," she said. "If you failed to notice, I haven't asked." Taking the last bite of her fritter, "I don't mean to sound like Mom," she uttered. "Without belaboring over this fairly distressing question - How she's doing?" "Call her, and ask for yourself? Better yet, why don't you visit? San Rafael is only a hop, skip, and jump from here."

"I would, if I thought there were the slightest chance that it would be pleasant." "Let her do all the talking," she suggested. "The last time that happened, I missed my exit." "That's not bad. Once in a while, everyone does that." "The next thing I knew, I saw a freeway sign that read, 'Welcome to Bakersfield,' she added in a disapproving manner. "What were you discussing?" "Ahh, what were we debating?" "And?" "It was concerning Nate. She stated, 'he's too skinny', and 'he should eat more beef and pork.'" "But you don't buy that type of meat." "Exactly." "Eugene would be climbing the walls, if he didn't have a steak over the weekend. And Mason's consumes cheeseburgers, French fries, and chocolate shakes like they're going out of style."

"Since I didn't turn out to be a boy..." Harri partially conveyed. "It's not your fault they omitted the plunger," she quipped. "I'll tell you, there were a couple of instances, where it would've came in handy," she jokingly said.

"Anyway, when Nate was in grade school, Mom had the gall to say that he was her son, and I was just a part-time, low wage guardian." "When she was babysitting Mason, she also flung the same tacky insult at me. Mom should've at least attempted to be more authentic," Carol undesirably mentioned. "When we were living here, and he was in pre-school, for a while, she agreed to take and pick him up during the week, except on Fridays. So I'd drop him off and they both understood that he didn't supposed to have or do specific things such as eat wheat cereal, drink sodas, or play on the grass too long due to his allergies. On our way home, he would provide me with a laundry list of things they did."

"Let me guess, it included every doggone thing that wasn't permissible," she presumed. "Yep. Then, I would call her and inquire." "What was her excuse?" she intriguingly asked. Get this - *I'm his Nana. Whenever he's with me, I have a right to care for him, however I see fit.'* "That's a show stopper." "According to her, they talk every day. Oh boy, and once he informs her that Linda is pregnant, I'm sure she'll smear my name to shreds. So I'm not calling or visiting her. And remember that you didn't see me," she inflexibly said. "So you want me to lie." "No, simply trim the fat." "Well, I call Mom every other evening, and visit on Sundays," she proudly declared. "And that makes you the chosen daughter."

Tugging on her split ends, "My impulse control is going to short circuit." Shaking her head, "I'm not fooling around this time. I feel like tearing off all my clothes!" Harri anxiously threatened. "Show off," she teased.

"Whew! Does this place serve spirits?" Without a response, she rapidly opened the menu, and pressed 'Service.' Shortly afterwards, Aaron returned, "Yes ladies?" Gesturing with her right index finger, "It's Aaron, correct?" "Yes, ma'am." "Do you sell liquor?" she optimistically inquired. "No." "Not even a light beer?" "Feeling under the weather, are we?" he hinted. Crazily eyeballing, "Miss Carol, you know we don't serve alcohol." "Trust me, I'm fully aware," she plainly said. Leaning across the table, "I'm assuming she's your sister. It's in your eyes," he said as he quickly glanced at them.

"Do you like Tequila?" "Who doesn't?" Harri snapped. "I have a bottle in my locker. I'll mix you up a small cocktail, but don't breathe a word." Grinning from ear to ear, "With a slice of lime, if you have it." Swirling and flipping his head backwards, "I feel a party coming on!" he exclaimed. "He's gay?" "Um hum." "On second thought, I like him. He's a cool dude." "He does possess a certain flair." "I'll make sure to leave him a good tip." "Save it. Besides driving a late model sports car, wearing the top of the line clothing, he'll be inheriting a small fortune when his parents either retire or pass away. Though, if he's like any other kid, he'll never be satisfied.

And that cynical notion, comes from several years of studying my own cunning children's behavior," Carol stated. Scanning around, "I wish there was a darn bell in here, because I would ring it twice. Once for you being an astute Mom; and secondly, for being a long-suffering daughter." Shrewdly, lifting her right eyebrow, "It's comforting to know we see eye-to-eye on something."

74

Chapter 7

<u>Mister Man Is Doubling Down</u>

Strutting into the patio area with an unique swagger was a burly gentleman, with big manly hands, salt and pepper hair; a bushy white mustache, wearing blue jeans, white long sleeved shirt, and a Lone Star belt; along with a caramel brown cowboy hat, matching boots, and dark sunglasses. He's also thought of as plain spoken, honest, and straightforward. Initially stunned, Harri zealously sprung out of her chair, ran over, and affectionately wrapped her arms around his football size neck, "Mister Man, you're here!" "In the flesh," he fun lovingly responded. "I'm so glad to see you," she said prior to planting one on his lips.

Standing back and taking an eye full, "Oooh wee, I almost didn't recognize you. You look fantastic!" Freely, pivoting his husky body, "You've noticed. It took me three months to lose sixteen pounds. You like?" "Yeah!" they both snapped. "I tried calling you. What's up with your phone numbers?" she asked. "My center is temporarily closed due to renovation. No use stock piling messages. So I let it ring. And I've changed my cell number, because Maya's family were constantly calling me. I'll text you with my new number."

"You don't want your wife contacting you?" Carol confusedly asked. "You didn't know. Four months ago, Maya left me for Palo, that (expletive) bum!" "Who's Palo?" "He was our roofing contractor," he replied as he used both hands to display quotation marks.

"Last month, I finally hired an attorney, and filed for an expensive divorce. Ugh! Shortly after our split, I stood in the bathroom mirror, evaluated my entire body, and thought, *'I don't blame her. Look at me. I've deserted myself.'* Then, I realized if I'm planning on returning to the dating scene, my gut needed to perform a disappearing act," he convincingly said. "Wait! You're getting a divorce?" "Harri knew." "Um hum." Gawking at her sister, "You never told me." "You never asked." "How do I suppose to ask, if you failed to provide a hint?"

Waving her off, "Mister Man, go on with what you were saying." Fingering his stomach, "While waiting in a unbelievably long checkout line at Rudy's Super Market, I read an article, which stated that some women are still attracted to men, who possesses a *'Dad's bod.'* That may be true, but at my age, I can't afford to bet against the odds. According to my doctor, and based on my height, I need to lose another thirty pounds."

"Are you on any specific diet plan?" Carol asked. "Yep! I can't have any breads, and I love cornbread. I could eat it every day," he gloomily mentioned. "In addition, I can't have pasta, potatoes, rice, beef, pork, gravy, fried food, cakes, cookies, pies, ice cream, juices, sodas, and anything else that's tasty. I've also joined a local fitness gym, and they've advised that I have to work out, at a minimum, one hundred and fifty (150) minutes per week. Currently, Linus, my trainer, is helping me to reach my goal." "You're looking mighty good," Harri happily commented. Zealously, raising his arms, "Wahoo! Well, alright!" he heartily shouted. "I've also stopped wearing black.

I hate to admit, but I was one of those folks who wore it on a regular basis, because I thought it made me look thinner. Now I am," he proudly stated. Pointing to a chair, "Won't you have a seat?" Carol suggested. "I can only stay a few minutes. I just came in for some coffee. This afternoon, I'm playing 'I Spy' on Otis, my underhanded contractor." "Before going on about a scheming scoundrel. I can't believe you're getting a divorce," she said. "Yeah, it wasn't my idea. Though, I should've saw it coming. Palo kept creeping by the house unannounced, saying he needed to check on something or other. The old rat (expletive)! Excuse me.

Originally, Maya and I agreed not to inform too many of our friends and family members regarding our decision. However, recently, I've discovered that only applied to my side. For some reason, my soon to be ex-in-laws are continuously bugging me about a whole lot of useless stuff." Taking a deep breath, "At least, the legal process is moving along fairly well," he confidently said. "I'm certain the entire ordeal is tiresome and undesirable. I hope everything works," Harri considerately conveyed. "Me too." "Thanks. Now back to that (expletive)." "Which one?" Carol quipped. "Huh, you're right. I could go on about both. Presently, I'm referring to Otis, the low down, mob boss. Every time we talk, he tells me about some (expletive) change order."

Gazing at Carol, "Lil sister, excuse my language. You and I have never spent any real time with each other. So I should warn you about my rough mannerism. For your sake, I'll try cleaning it up." "Okay." "Back to what I was saying, that (expletive) makes me hot under the collar!

I know it's his way of sticking it to me, and padding the #$@^&% bill." Staring at Harri, "We're in the wrong racket," he earnestly stated. "I hear you. Are you doing an expansion? Because the last time I visited your place, there was a lot of foot traffic." Flipping open the menu, "Yep. I'm doubling down. Last year, I purchased the adjacent vacant lot. I'm planning on adding a skating disco. Ross, a good friend, and business associate, have been successfully betting on hunches for the past twenty years. Besides his men's clothing store, he also own residential property in Berkeley, Marin, Napa, and Upper Rockridge (Oakland). With those four holdings alone, he's a multi-millionaire, and sharp as a whip." As an afterthought, "Ahh, I'll skip a second cup," he mumbled.

"What was I saying? Um, yes, presently, he and his wife are vacationing in Europe. Before they left, we went to lunch, and he projected anything to do with discos were going to make a profitable comeback. We figured these kids aren't sporting Afros and wearing platform shoes for nothing. We're also tossing around the idea of a partnership." Staring directly at him, "Mister Man, do you really want that?" Harri doubtfully inquired. "Hum, we'll see. Anyhow, since I'm a bit older than both of you, I vividly recall the 70's, and I know exactly how the renovation should look." "Is everything running smoothly?" Carol inquired.

"Overall, I would say so. However, in passing, Otis mentioned that he ran into a minor stumbling block. He's having difficulties locating one of those gigantic disco balls. You know, the kind that hangs from the middle of the dance floor.

Heck, if it comes to, I'll have my daughter make one out of Paper Mache, that'll save some moola. Hum, maybe after I leave here, I'll stop by a few thrift stores," he said. Widely grinning, "Boy, if I'm able to make a go of this, I'll retire in five years." "You're solely banking on your friend's opinion?" Carol burbled. "Lil sister, I know what you're driving at. Disco in the 21st Century? Yeah, it's chancy. However, if Plan A goes south, which it shouldn't, but if it does, I have Plan B and C standing by," he answered.

Eyeing Harri, "As you previously observed, we've also outgrown our existing space. If all three of my plans fail, I'll lease out the expansion. Either way, I know the U.C. Berkeley kids will continue patronizing my arcade center. I've also been mulling over the idea of featuring a live band every weekend. Heck, I may even add a grill. For the past six years, I've been itching to modify my business model." "No risk, no reward," Harri said. "It's the only way to boogie," he added with a chuckle. Shrewdly, peering at Harri, "Don't even try sugar coating your situation." "Let me guess. She has fallen madly in love with a jailbird," he good-humoredly jested. Consequently, they remained silent. "Can't you gals take a joke?" Prior to sipping, "He's clairvoyant," Carol murmured.

Interrupting their discussion, Aaron approached, "We didn't have any lemons or limes on hand. So I added a splash of lemonade." "Cool." Snatching the cloudy drink, "Let me sample that, before you slobber in it," Carol playfully expressed. "It's only after my fifth, that I start modestly slobbering. Thank you very much." Prior to leaving, "Hey kid, make sure to check on us every five minutes," Harri requested.

"Young fella, bring me one, and filled the glass with ice. I like mines chilled." Spiritedly, pointing one finger in the air, "*Parteeee*," he funnily sang. As usual, when it comes to women and your exclusive society, I need a smart chip." "No, Duke, you hit the bullseye," Carol said. Taking a couple of gulps, "There is a GOD," Harri pleasurably uttered. "What's going on?" he asked. "Nothing much, except Carol has duly appointed herself as my alternate mother. Like the first one wasn't damaging enough." "Girlie, you know darn well, it is bad juju dating Hambone. So I have no choice, but to act as your moral compass," she firmly conveyed.

Bewilderedly gazing, "I'm lost. Are we speaking about a dude who loves collard greens or pinto beans cooked with ham?" "No, he's a sleazy polecat," Carol sharply replied. "When I met him, I wasn't aware of his criminal history." "And yet when you became fully abreast, you failed to act accordingly," she countered. Gawking at both sisters, "Are you gals pulling my leg, or what?" he asked. "No, we're not," Carol uttered. Peering in Harri's direction, "Are you experiencing a serious rift in your marriage?" "The size of a crater," she quipped. "Riggs is out?" "And they claim you're slow." "Huh, I thought you had Riggs on lock down. Did he run off for a night with a sexy cocktail waitress?" he oddly asked.

"Uh-uh." "Then, he must have done something really dastardly." "It's what he hasn't done is the true backstory." Right away, several creases appeared across his forehead, "Since I was smacked over the head with the same dreadful accusation, let me proceed further down the road," he uneasily said.

"How did you meet, um, your latest numero uno? When did you start seeing him? And what was his crime of choice?" Purposely, avoiding eye contact, "I met him on a dating website, and we've been seeing each other for almost three weeks, and his prior offense was burglary." Harshly, squinting his eyes, "Ugh! I despise burglars. They're such a messy bunch," he growled. Contemplating for a moment, "Didn't we talk two weeks ago? I specifically recalled asking you how everything was going, and you didn't spill a bean." "I wasn't ready." "Fair enough. This is what I know. You're not in love, because you haven't spent enough time with him.

And if I know you, you're managing a compressed work schedule possibly three/twelves or four/tens," he presumed. "Three/twelves and sometimes a little overtime." Caressing his mustache, "Every time I'm waiting in any check-out line, I'll usually pick up one of those gossip magazines. I don't have enough fingers and toes to describe how often I've read a starlet saying, *'it was love at first sight.'* Gals, I'm not trying to be sexist, but men don't think or speak that way, unless they're coached. Or she'll proclaim that Mr. Wonderful is her *'soul mate.'* Whatever in the hell that means. No matter what anyone says, I know for certain true love grows over time, similar to a stock portfolio. Anything else, your sexual glands are screwing with you," he advised.

In an accusatory tone, "What was the cause of your divorce?" Harri asked. "Don't look at me cockeyed, like I'm some dumb chump. I didn't stray with a dame over the weekend.

Though, on one rare occasion, I was fairly tempted. Generally, I took Maya for granted, and we're all guilty of that. There were also too many broken promises, late nights, and cancelled dates, due to my business is my first wife. But it wasn't a total loss. We stayed married for fifteen years, and brought into this madcap world, one bright, giddy, and adorable baby girl." "What's her name?" Carol asked. "Rosa. She was named after Maya's mother. Interestingly, the sweet old broad past away in her sleep, two days before our Rosa was born. Amazing, how things work out, isn't it? The elderly moves onward, and shortly afterwards, a new one arrives." "It makes you wonder," Carol uttered. "We also created some unforgettable memories. I can't tell you how many times, I've bumped into an old friend, or chatted with a stranger, who told me that I was fortunate.

It wasn't until I packed my bags, when it hit me that all Maya wanted was to spend some quality time with me." "That's terrible," Harri chirped. "Dixon has been my business manager for several years, and he does a terrific job. If I was wiser, I should've shoved three quarters of the responsibility over to him, spent less time at the shop, and more with my family," he candidly professed. "Is it too late to reconcile?" Carol subtly asked. "Yep, the stallion has bolted from the barn."

"Mister Man, I know exactly how your wife felt. All of you workaholic husbands need to re-establish your priorities. I understand some men have a vision, but there's other aspects in life that requires the same amount of attention.

In addition, whenever you're at home, put a lid on the J-O-B, because it's tiresome, endless, and boring. You also need to be a willing participant in your own (expletive) marriage, without being continuously coerced to do so," Harri strongly stated. "That's what I don't like about women. A dude can openly admit that he was dead wrong, and you're still hammering the coffin shut." Wagging his right index finger, "Sometimes you women are a big distraction. But I can't give you up, because you're soft and you smell too good," he said with a grin. "Keep in mind, we have to nag, because you guys are only using half a brain," Harri coldly countered. "Duke, before you arrived, I've been trying to talk some sense into her. As usual, we have conflicting ideas. Overall, she believes I'm trying to restrict her freedom," Carol said.

"And I've been reassuring her that I got this. As far as I'm concern, we've been unnecessarily dueling." Flexing her right hand, "You've got nothing. You're driving on a perilous collision course, with grief flagging you up ahead. Basically, I'm strongly recommending that she eliminate her so-called midnight madness rendezvouses with Hambone." "Carol, stop saying that," she said. "I get it. You two are gridlocked. Let me take a stab at this," he said. Demonstrating with his fingers, "First, once you end a long term relationship or marriage, give yourself plenty of downtime. Take minimally a year, prior to beginning a new one. Nothing good ever comes from being too hasty.

Secondly, don't ever hook up with a fella who has nothing to lose, because he's a stone loser," he said as he flashed an L underneath his brim.

I got that zany symbol from Rosa. She makes it every time she considers someone to be shady. Thirdly, don't ever let yourself go as I did, because you won't gain anything except regret and frequent heartburn. I hope I don't forget to cover this important topic, whenever she starts dating. I don't want my baby girl to fall for a bum, a fella with no ambition. Then, later, I'll find her gorging on some high calorie junk food, because he decided to dump her."

With her lips tightened, Harri briskly climbed out of her chair, rushed over, and stood near the patio entry, "Where's that darn kid?" she eagerly questioned with her hands placed firmly on her hips. "Okay! He hit one out the park. Don't get upset. If we didn't care, we wouldn't take the time," she caringly professed. Balling up his right fist, and lifting it mid-air, "Right on!" Boldly, sashaying towards their table, "Look here, Mister Man, you're my best friend, at least I presumed you were. Why are you cosigning her? And Carol, I guess I was under the false impression that we were supposed to be catching up. Instead I feel like we've been playing pool, but rather than being an opponent, I'm the (expletive) cue ball. Or does this represent an intervention?" she upsettingly inquired.

Swirling around in her seat, "For the life of me, I can't fathom why you're so defensive about some down-and-out scum bag, you hardly know?" "Yeah, we're only trying to help. Don't treat us like we're simple-minded terrorists posing as relatives from an apocalyptic planet." "That's a weird combo of words," Carol peculiarly commented. Titling his hat, "What can I tell you, I'm into Sci-Fi."

Chapter 8

You Ought To Know Better

Flopping into her chair, "Ugh! Could we drop it? I have enough going on without considering reconciling with someone, who's much too busy to even inform me that our son's girlfriend is pregnant," she irritatingly declared. Eyebrows raised, "Stop the presses! Holy cow! Nate is becoming a father? When did that happen?" he eagerly asked. Seething in anger, "Shut up, Mister Man!" "Now you're thin skinned?" Carol countered. Scratching his chin, "Why are we digging through your dirty laundry, anyway?" he grumbled. Suddenly, a recipient of a spiteful stare, "Am I being too blunt?"

"Oooh, and she also contends that Riggs is attempting to poison her with a new brand of toothpaste," she abruptly shared. "What?" "Look, I'm willing to discuss that..." she partially conveyed. "It's outright preposterous, isn't it?" Carol asserted. In an eerie tone, "As hefty and strong, as Riggs is, if he truly wanted to do away with you, it would only require one precise snap of your sensual and extremely fragile neck," he said as he touched one side. *'Gulp,'* Carol nervously reacted. "You're morbid," Harri snapped.

Thumbing his chest, "Me? You're the one insinuating that your husband, who adores the very ground you walk on, is planning on committing a calculated and gruesome murder. What a disturbing accusation. It makes me wonder whether you're misusing prescription drugs," he glumly said.

"I am not! In my defense, not too long ago, I bought four tubes of toothpaste, and placed them in the hall closet. Somehow, they've all vanished. Where did they disappear to? That's what I would like to know. And where in the hell did that worthless toothpaste in a can come from? It makes me queasy every time I've used it," she whined. "I could've sworn three grown people including one energetic dog, who believes he's part human, presently lives in your home. Then, there's your son's girlfriend, and a few of his pals who also frequently visits. Have you checked with any of them?" he sensibly inquired. "No, not yet." "Maybe it's a practical joke, and you're not in on it," he rationally suggested. "In any case, you ought to know better. Riggs isn't about that." "I agree," Carol uttered.

Innocently, peering around, Harri failed to offer any other defense. "This subject is awfully distasteful. Could we move onto a more realistic, and less fascinating subject?" he asked. Pivoting in her seat, "I second that," Carol snapped. "Where in the heck is that kid?" Not a minute too soon, "Sorry, I took so long. I decided to make a pitcher, instead of a single serving." "Excellent timing my man." Observing two extra glasses on the tray, "Say, what's up?" Harri asked. "Aaron, you can return them. I just wanted to taste hers, and I'm driving," she said.

Leaning forward, "Miss Carol, could I crash your party?" he whispered. "How old are you?" "Last month, I turned twenty one." Swigging the cocktail, "If the kid wanted to, he could be a decent bartender. Check his identification, and if he's not fibbing, he can stay, as long as he keeps his lips buttoned," she determined.

Hurriedly, he retrieved his driver's license, displayed it, and untied his apron, "You won't hear a peep." "When are you off?" Carol asked. Verifying the time and pulling up a chair, "In exactly twenty seconds......I'm done!" Pouring some of the refreshment into his glass, "It's been ages since I had some downhome lemonade," Duke eagerly mentioned. Taking a big gulp, "Aww! It's spiked!" Clearing his throat, "What's in this crud?" Giggling out loud, "That's what you get!" Harri teased. In a hoarse voice, "You should've given this old crow a heads up. Aww! My throat is (inaudible)."

"Oooh wee, you're turning an irresistible blood red," she added. Casually, sipping his drink, "So what are we discussing?" Aaron smoothly inquired. "Remember," Carol whispered. Frowning into his glass, "*Pardon*," he replied with an imitation French accent. Out of left field, "Aaron! Aaron!" a strong male voice echoed from the café. Immediately, he crouched down into his chair. "Who's that?" Harri asked. "My manic-depressive father." Suddenly, a slender, mature gentleman, with gray hair walked towards their table. "There you are. Hi Carol," he cordially acknowledged. "John." "Son, you forgot to put away the produce shipment. You better get a move on. Folks, I apologize for the interruption." Once Aaron was within arms-length distance, "You've been drinking??" he furiously shouted. "Dad, let me explain!" he cried out. "Uh-oh," Harri murmured. "For some reason, once that kid joined our hillbilly soiree, a pesky voice inside of my head kept saying, *'You'll be sorrrry,'* Duke quietly wisecracked.

"Shut up Aaron! And do what I've asked!" "Carol, the last time we spoke, I privately shared with you that he possessed two significant behavioral challenges.

One was his lack of maturity. The second one I purposely withheld, because I was too embarrassed. Nonetheless, based on my reaction, I'm presuming you've gleaned what the second one is." Grimacing and nodding, "In any case, I'll spell it out for you. Aaron also has a serious drinking problem, and we've been trying to convince him to join AA (Alcohol Anonymous)." "John, we didn't mean any harm."

Transiently, glancing into the cafe, "For crying out loud, you're a mother. Clearly, I wrongfully assumed that you understood. Nonetheless, I have no choice but to ban you and your merry drunken comrades from my establishment." Promptly, everyone stood up and gathered their belongings. Gingerly, touching his shoulder, "I'm truly sorry. He was with us for less than a minute," Carol regrettably conveyed. "And he would've stayed longer, if I wasn't searching for him. He just turned twenty one, and that's not my only concern. My business could get shut down for serving alcohol on the premises. I don't have a liquor license!" he angrily advised.

Tilting sideways towards Harri, "What a fine mess. Now I'll have to scratch this place," Duke quietly griped. Pondering over the situation, *I've been thrown out of a couple of chintzy bars, but never a Café. I'm responsible for that kid getting into trouble with his Dad. Woo, I've hit an all-time low. I hope Carol doesn't reveal that I'm a cop,'* she thought.

"You know, my sister is..," Offhandedly, she felt something prodding her. Strolling towards the exit, "Yes, she's her older sister, and I'm their first cousin. We're awfully sorry. Let's go gals."

"Aren't you the owner of Far-Out?" John suspiciously inquired. Swiftly, yanking his hat over his brows, "Uh, no, but I know who you're speaking of. He's a hell of a cool cat," he sheepishly responded. Pointing towards the sliding glass doors, "Out! And don't ever come back! If I receive a violation, you'll be hearing from my attorney! Aaron, where are you??" Once they reached outside, "Wow, that dude got a set of lungs on him," Harri remarked. "You can say that again," he said.

Positioned directly in front of them, "Wait a cotton pickin minute! Why did you guys find it necessary to shoved me out the (expletive) door?" "You cursed?" "Yes!" "Carol, you didn't know how to back the play," she said. "Since we're all swearing sailors, I'm curious, before ushering you off the premises, what were you going to say?" Duke doubtfully asked. "I forgot. But it wasn't what you guys thought," she self-consciously answered. "If we're going to get mashed, I'll require something much stronger. Let's head over to the Linden's Room," he proposed. "The one in El Cerrito? I thought you had something better to do," Carol mockingly stated. "I did. But hanging with you two reminds me of my early college days. Getting kicked out of a place, with liquor on our breaths, banned for life, that brought back some fond memories," he happily expressed.

"Mister Man, I'm delighted you found that scene hysterical. The only part that wasn't cool, he threaten to sue us," Harri mentioned. "He won't. I know John. He was probably more upset with Aaron's behavior. If it was just us three drinking, he would've just provided a stern warning. But he wouldn't have blew up like that," she explained.

"How about it? But we'll have to take one of your vehicles, because I purposely parked several blocks away, in order to burn some calories." "I'm driving a Tahoe. We'll take mine. It's not too far from here," Harri offered. "I'm surprised you rented a truck," she said. "I'm not. I prefer something big and sturdy." As they strolled along the crowded avenue, they teased each other about the incident, and Carol mentioned that she'll forward an apology letter next week.

Approaching Dwight Way, "See the silver truck, parked in front of the yellow beetle (Volkswagen) bus - that's it." "Hand me the keys, you're loaded. Though, I had the same, I only tasted it. Tequila is cool for parties, but it's not my first choice. However, if the kid slid over some corn whiskey, we would definitely need car service," he said. Shortly afterwards, they headed down Telegraph Avenue towards the University of California Berkeley campus. Gazing out of the rear passenger's window, "We're leaving with no time to spare. It's almost 3:00 o'clock, and everyone is going home," Carol remarked. Unexpectedly, the vehicle sputtered and stalled near a busy intersection. Attempting to crank the engine, "What in the hell is going on?" he growled.

Propping forward from the rear seat, "Duke, look at the gauge. Are we out of gas? Or does it register empty, because the engine is off?" Carol asked. In a nonchalant manner, "I don't have the faintest idea," Harri arrogantly chimed in. "Turn the key again," Carol advised. Once it confirmed her suspicion, "Shoot! We're done for!" "Do it again," Harri prompted. To no avail, he complied. Tipping his brim upward, and examining the gauge, "We're out gas??"

"I don't know," she gullibly whined. Gripping the dashboard, "*Grrr,* what kind of hare-brained car-rental operation gives their customer a vehicle without any fuel?" "Where's your agreement?" she inquired. "I don't know! Why?" she annoyingly shouted. *['HONK, HONK, HONK!!']*. "Look inside the glove box!" Carol urged. Immediately, she opened the compartment, discovered a pink invoice, and tossed it to her, "Knock yourself out."

Studying the invoice, "There's a diagram, which shows how much gas the truck had, when you received it. According to this, it possessed less than an eighth of a tank. You must have taken the city streets from Oakland to here. Good night! How could you've overlooked the stupid gauge? It's in plain view. Were you literally sleep at the wheel?" she frustratingly questioned. Flipping her hand in mid-air, "Could you chill?" Harri shouted. "We wouldn't be in this outrageous predicament, with everyone honking, shouting, and giving us the finger, if you concentrated on anything remotely substantive!" she ranted. Waving his hands in a frenzy, "Gals, gals, as much as I love watching boxing, we need to get the heck out of here!"

Pivoting in his seat, "Lil sister, scoot your narrow behind up here, and call roadside service. Tell them, we're out of gas," he urged. Staring at Harri, "Meanwhile, you and I will manage the rear." *['HONK, HONK, HONK!!!']* Scanning the area, "Where? Every (expletive) parking space is taken!" Peering up the street, "At the end of the block, there's a red curb that's open. Unless you prefer to wait for an imaginary action hero to save us, I suggest we get to stepping.

C'mon, quick stalling! Lil sister, did you catch all of that?" he agitatedly asked. Grabbing her purse from the back seat, "Check!" Climbing out the front passenger side, *'This vehicle has been badly rained on, and it's huge. I'm wearing two different size boots, and now my clothes are going to become filthy. What's the (expletive) point?'* she exasperatingly thought. Heavy-handedly, slamming the door, and stomping towards the rear, "This is so $#@^&%*!" Strangely, gazing at her, "What's up with the your (expletive) attitude? Give it all you got, when I say GO!" he zealously instructed. "Ugh!"

Chapter 9

<u>Evaluating The Sister's Marriages</u>

Leaning against the rear bumper, "Lil sister, place it in neutral, and whatever you do, don't stop, until we reach the red curb! Motorists will get the picture! You got me?" he yelled. Straightaway, she extended her left hand out of the window, and made an '*OK*' gesture. Glancing to his right, "Remember to put your back into it!" Prior to his signal, she took a deep breath. "GO!" All of the sudden, two young men walking down the same side of the street, noted their predicament and readily assisted.

After they made a final shove towards the appointed spot, they waved and continued on their way. "Thanks guys!" Duke shouted. "Yeah baby! I just shaved five minutes off my workout," he gratefully stated with perspiration glistening from his hands. Observing Carol's movements inside the cab, "Good. She's on the phone with a towing service." "Mister Man, I haven't ran out of gas since I was in my early twenties. Do me a favor, don't tell her, but she was right. My mind has been too preoccupied with things of no real importance, and that's dangerous in my line of work," Harri wearily stated.

Popping out of the driver's side, "Hey ya'll, we're in luck! A tow truck is within the vicinity. According to the dispatcher, they received a call from a guy who needed a jump, but when their driver arrived, the motorist was nowhere to be found," she conveyed.

"He must have gotten help from someone else," Harri presumed. "That's what the dispatcher thought. Who cares? Otherwise, we would be stranded for at least an hour, if not more." "All of this huffing and puffing has triggered my appetite," he said. "Is 'Berkeley's Best Dogs' located in the same spot?" Harri asked. "Yep. Sounds like a wiener," he quipped. "I'm game," Carol chimed in. "Once we get some gas, let's move the truck, and walk over there," he suggested. "Cool." A few minutes later, Carol pointed up the street, spotted the tow truck, and enthusiastically waved, "That's our guy! Yahoo!" After double parking, a middle aged, male, who wore dark blue coveralls, jumped out the cab, "I heard you folks ran out of gas," he politely said. "Yes!"

Right away, he worked his way underneath the hood, then switched over to the rear of his vehicle, and quickly retrieved a one gallon gas can. "I'll have you guys rolling in no time." "We appreciate your assistance, Mr. Tow Man," Carol flirtatiously remarked. With a subtle wink, "Anything for a beautiful lady." Sidestepping towards Harri, "Don't you love men who works with their hands?" she whispered. "It also doesn't hurt that he has come to our rescue." Six minutes later, "Okay, you're all set." "He's wonderful," Carol uttered.

"Folks, I'll be in the area for at least a half an hour. I have another call on Shattuck Avenue. If you have any other problems with your vehicle, feel free to call me," he said as he handed her a business card. Patting on his back, "You bet," Duke snapped. "We're grateful for your speedy service," Harri gratefully expressed. "You're our hero!" Carol chimed in.

While watching him merging into oncoming traffic, "You were on the prowl." Friskily, fanning her face with his card, "No I wasn't. Just verifying whether I still knew how to flirt," she explained. "Alright gals, that's enough plotting. Let's mosey out of this red zone, and find a legal parking space." Shortly afterwards, they observed a long line that snaked more than half a block from the popular eatery. Marveling at the number of patrons waiting, "Is it always this way?" Harri asked. "Once the tourists caught on, they became more popular than ever," Carol replied. "You want to wait or what?" Duke inquired. "We're here. Let's wait." "Okay, before we discontinue discussing the life and times of Harri, I wanted to say one last thing," he said. "And then, that's it. Finito." "Guaranteed." "We've been friends for almost twenty years, and I love you because you're like my kinfolks. But you have one weak trait that I've never cared for."

"I'm better at Texas Hold'em?" she teased. "Nope. But I'll add that to my mounting list. Essentially, once you've made a decision, you become stubborn, which is unfortunate because there's some areas in life that demands further consideration, and your long term marriage is one of them," he explained. "So that's where Bonnie got that from," Carol murmured. "In my opinion, you need to mull over the idea of getting a divorce. No one is perfect, and Riggs hasn't cheated on you, which typically tops the chart. Unless I'm wrong?" "No, you're not," she replied. "I pretty much alluded to the same thing," Carol chirped.

"Since his plate is overflowing with working as a Watch Commander, serving in the U.S. Army Reserves every other weekend, and volunteering at the shelter.

Oh, and let's not forget, or grinding away on a home improvement project, he's probably coming across as someone who's not willing to compromise. At the end of a long and exhausting week, an abominable sea creature would be considered a more suitable companion." "You got that right." "So you get that he's mentally strapped, and he doesn't mean you any harm?" he straightforwardly asked. "Maybe."

"Harri, you're the mother of his child, best friend, counselor, backup partner if necessary, and the lady he chose to marry. This is the time when he needs you the most. Instead of penalizing him, you should be helping him. He understands what's happening within the mechanics of your marriage, but he's overwhelmed. So he's depending on you to shore up the rear, and hoping you'll start offering solutions. You've been on this page before. What's different?" he supportively asked. "I don't know. I guess I'm tired of playing the heavy."

Placing his right hand on her shoulders, "Or are you tired of being married?" "No," she timidly replied. Gawking and pointing at her, "Oooh, you are!" Carol said. "I don't have to tell you the field is crowded with a bunch of messy divorcees," Duke said with a frown. "Oodles!" "Speaking of dealing with someone else's baggage. Whew!" he added. "I know," she uttered. "Personally, I have the wherewithal to become joined at the hip with my mate for life, but Maya felt differently. One time, we were quarreling over Rosa's middle school grades, and she shouted, '*I hate being married!*' After nine years of marriage, that was the first time she ever made such a hurtful statement. It hit me like a ton of bricks. Not in my wildest dreams, could I've imagined saying anything remotely like that to her.

Needless to say, it was a frightening reminder that a love one can drastically change their mind, and say, *'It is over,'* at the drop of a hat. If you decide to get a divorce, who's next? Even a more intelligent question is – What's next? Another fella on the force, who's a major cheater. Then, a second divorce? Where does it end? C'mon, you need to give it another try," he encouraged. "I have." "Then, try again, I did. Perhaps, the next time, you'll sound more encouraging, and he'll be intently listening. And by all means, don't try to have a conversation when you're hotter than a flame thrower. That's a waste of time and energy. Sometimes the best couples can become lost in their own private world." "Ain't that the truth," Carol chirped.

"In addition, if you really want your marriage to work, they'll be those occasions when you'll have to contribute more than usual. Clearly, this could be one of those times." "I'm on that page," Carol admitted. "Prior to relocating to Southern California, Riggs visited my center, and we talked for over an hour. In the midst of our discussion, he openly shared his love for you and your family. I have to tell you, not too many dudes are willing to that, unless he's on a highly rated game show," he quipped. "He did?" she unknowingly asked. "Um hum. Prior to leaving, we shook hands and wished each other well. Harri, your husband is a stand-up dude. Overall, I'm certain filing for a divorce wasn't his idea," he presumed. "Does it matter?" she nonchalantly asked. "Yes, it does!" Carol snapped.

"You're a fine couple, with a lot going on, and that's rare. Give yourselves a break. Take a world wind vacation, you guys can afford it. When you return, I'm sure you would've ironed out the kinks.

Harri, your marriage could use some tweaking, but it's totally workable," he sagely advised. Scratching the top of her head, "Mister Man, did you graduate in family psychology?" "No, just common sense. Why do you think I waited before I filed for a divorce?" "I hear you," she reflectively uttered. Peering over in Carol's direction, "Lil sister, how's life treating you?" he asked. "Oooh, I get a turn. Great! Number one, Eugene, my husband, is a complete jerk! He has been cheating on me and missing some important family functions. Secondly, Bonnie, my teenage daughter, isn't certain what ethnicity she wants to be during any given time.

Thirdly, Mason, my son, has been callously sleeping with numerous girls, and one had to be hospitalized, due to depression. I also believe that he's increasing his chances of contracting a venereal disease. Last but not least, next week, I have my first appointment with a shrink. Other than that, everything is fine," she clumsily answered. Ogling at Harri, "Do you have a giant paper clip?" "No, why?" "So I can clamp my fat lips shut," he regretfully replied. "Duke, I openly invite your opinion. Generally, Eugene makes me feel like I'm either exaggerating or imagining things." Scanning their surroundings, "Go ahead Mister Man. Everybody seems to be talking among their selves. They don't know us anyway," Harri mentioned.

Meanwhile, two strangers who were standing a few feet away began whispering. "That was fair-minded," one said. "So far. Now he's going to analyze the shorter one, and she's loaded to the gills. A sleaze ball for a husband, and a mood swinging teenaged daughter. She can take my turn. To me, her son sounds normal.

When I was in my early twenties, I was also considered a tiger in a tank," the other funnily remarked. "You still are." "I'll take that as a compliment." "Shhh, let's hear what he has to say."

"Lil sister, last year, your husband and a couple of his co-workers also visited my place, and he recognized me. So we chatted for a few minutes. Later that summer, I accompanied Dad to the DMV (Department of Motor Vehicles), and I ran into him again. Since we were a captive audience, we tossed around varied topics. Somehow we landed on the subject of childhood experiences, and he openly shared that he was raised by his Mom, a single parent, had a *'fatherless life,'* and *'it was no big deal,'* he said. "Eugene has always been cavalier about that aspect of his life," Carol shared. "On our way home, Dad said, *'Poor kid, I'm sure his family suffered.'*

In sharp contrast, I grew up in a *'Leave It to Beaver'* household, with very few exceptions. Nothing much happened, unless one of us stepped out of line. Then, Mom would get riled up. She was the disciplinarian among my parents. The next day, I checked on Dad, and we revisited that discussion, and he said, *'Son, in those days, without a decent job, it was tough making ends meet.'* Later, that evening, I was going over some figures, when I overheard my daughter and her kooky friend's proposing to place some gooey marshmallows on top of their cupcakes, in order to see if they would *'pop off.'* Of course, my wife was standing nearby, supervising their baking operation. Harri, you know I didn't finish college," he said. "Yep, me too."

"Afterwards, while taking a showered, I wondered, if I didn't get a substantial loan from Dad, how would I've supported us?" "You could've applied with SCPD." "Law enforcement isn't my thing," Duke said. "You're big and strong. How about working in construction?" Carol suggested. "Uh-uh. I guess my point is sometimes harsh circumstances can prevent a guy from becoming a loving husband and father. A man has his pride, you know." "I see what you mean. Possibly, Eugene's father wanted to be part of their life, but he was ashamed, because he couldn't financially afford to do so. So he stayed away," she reasonably speculated. "Um hum." "Is Gina his first indiscretion?" he uncomfortably asked.

Without a response, Harri became flustered, "Answer him." Spontaneously, Carol hunched over, covered her face, and miserably cried. Startled by her reaction, "You mean that son of a (expletive) has been cheating on you the entire time?" Briskly, exposing her sopping face, "Yes! Ever since we've been married." Straightening her posture and wiping her eyes, "Lord knows, I'm a plain person with ordinary goals." Brushing up against Duke's right arm, and sharply contorting her lips, "Stand by, here comes a testimony," Harri murmured. "Is there a chicken exit?" he inventively whispered. "Uh-uh."

"...in my family, we're considered blessed if we can afford a new car every ten years; replace a window in our old drafty house, and that's only if Eugene receives an annual bonus; buy the kids some new school clothes for the fall term; or purchase a new ice hockey uniform and equipment for Mason.

On a weekly basis, I'm also inclined to compare the price of food among a variety of super markets. That's the world I live in. I'll never save someone's life, restore order in a crime infested community, or arrest a drug dealer who's selling to vulnerable children. Nor will I ever build a successful business. Deep down, managing my family's life is all I know," she agonizingly professed. "Boy, she's preachy. For a moment, I thought she was going to pass around a collection plate," he wisecracked. "Carol, we get it. But why did you keep his adulterous ways concealed all these years?" "Would it have made a difference?" she derisively questioned.

With a stunned expression, "Yes, it would've. You're my sister. You and the kids could've left him, and moved in with us. We would've figured things out," she frankly answered. "I didn't want to burden you." "I'll be right back." Immediately, Harri rushed through the line, ran inside the eatery, and grabbed a few napkins. Upon return, "Here, wipe your face," she caringly instructed. "Gals, let me continue, before my mind wanders off. These days, it'll do that without advanced warning," he said. "Please go on." "How long have you been married?" he asked. "Almost nineteen years." "Mister Man, there's something else important...," Harri partially conveyed.

Swiveling his hulking body, "Ease up, will you." "Lil sister, you've tried your best, and perhaps he tried his, but it appears that he's incapable of changing his behavior. By all account, you've forgiven him for the length of your marriage, and I commend you." Bouncing in place, "I have to say it," Harri impatiently mumbled. Tilting his hat, "Go ahead."

"I was trying to tell you that his (expletive) mistress is pregnant." Staring at Carol, "Lil sister is that true?" Pathetically, lowering her head, "Yes." "What kind of sick game is Eugene playing? Sexual roulette? You have to let the (expletives) go!" he resolutely declared. Acknowledging her pain, "Again, I apologize. I knew this subject was similar to pushing an alert button, and we're still standing in line," he said while peeking over his shoulders. "In regards to Bonnie, all kids come up with some mindboggling notions. So don't let that bother you. Since she spends so much time in school, get in touch with her guidance counselor. Over the years, I've discovered they have a different spin on our kids.

More than likely, her pseudo identity crisis is behind some stinky boy. In terms of Mason, as long as he suits up, if you know what I mean, and be upfront with all of his sexual partners, everyone should be fine," he advised. Closer to the entrance, "Awesome. We're almost inside," Harri cheerfully announced.

Meanwhile the same two strangers began sharing their opinion, "So what do you think?" he whispered to his male companion. "Okay, you're fond of the big lug. In an attempt to avoid a delicious, but ludicrous argument, I agree that he does sound sensible. However, you'll have to admit, the taller lady is aiming to kick the living daylights out of someone. Did you see how she was bobbing in place?" "Um hum. For all we know, she could be a man-eater. We better keep our distance," he whispered as they both took a step backwards.

Unexpectedly, Carol fell into his arms and cried, *'Awww, Awww.'* Patting her shoulder, "Lil sister, it'll all work out. You'll see. Time heals all things." Agitatedly, shaking her head, "I knew it! I knew she would breakdown at this precise moment." "I don't want a hot dog!!" she loudly cried. "Well, I (expletive) do!" Harri declared. Instantaneously, many of the patrons standing nearby possessed a befuddled look, "What's wrong with the freakin hot dogs?" someone restlessly shouted. Approaching the cashier, "Welcome to Berkeley's Best Dogs, what would you like?" a male associate courteously asked.

Slapping a fifty on top of the counter, "I'll have a fat German Frankfurter on a wheat bun, and a diet coke." "Make that two," Duke said. Staring at Carol, "Is she alright? Does she need some water?" he considerately asked. "Naw! She's full of drama and the usual crapola," Harri roughly responded. Within earshot distance, "For the love of GOD, give her some water!" someone bitterly cried out. Swirling around, "Shut up, whoever you are! She's my younger sister! And I can mistreat her all I want!" "Don't be so insensitive," another remarked. Sneering at Harri and signaling the associate, "Man, give me some water," Duke quietly requested. "Right away, sir."

"By golly, I've put up with her, *'I need to embarrass my older sister in public routine, for over twenty years.'* This time, I'm not falling for it," she quietly grumbled. Seconds later, he extended a small water cup, and politely said, "Here you go, miss." "You're a gentleman." "It was my pleasure. AL-righty! We'll have your orders ready in a jiffy!"

Standing within close proximity, "Say, what's up with the hulk and those two ladies?" a different stranger inquired. "Ever since we've been in line, the taller chick and her boyfriend have been piling up on the smaller one," one of the eavesdroppers advised. Pivoting and leaning inward, "We've been listening off and on for a while, and they don't necessarily give a rat's (expletive) about men either," the other persuasively whispered.

Observing Duke reaching into his rear pants pocket, "Mister Man, I got it. You're still coddling." "Love you too," he quipped. Blowing her nose, "I don't know how ya'll can eat and joke at a time like this," she cried. Biting into her plump hot dog, "No sweat," Harri garbled. While the trio were huddled in a nearby corner, she shoved some of the frankfurter near her sister's mouth, "Take a bite. You'll feel better," she convincingly advised. "Um hum."

Chapter 10

Three Synchronized Heroes

As recommended, Carol nibbled on the last of Harri's hot dog. "Um, that's tasty. Order me one." "Sorry babe, I can't cut the line. We'll pick you up something else." "We should shove off," Duke said. Once they reached outside, [Cell phone rang], "It's me," she snapped. "This is Harri." "Good afternoon Detective Wilburn, this is Detective Ivan Olson from LAPD's Internal Affairs Division (IAD). Am I reaching you at an inconvenient time?" he considerately asked. "No, go right ahead." "It's my understanding that you're managing a case in the Bay Area, with the assistance of the Oakland Police Department."

"That's correct. Brock, my partner, and I are both here." "Is he with you?" Consequently, she fearfully thought, *'Geez! LAPD stumbled across something against bonehead. But why would their IAD be contacting me? Whatever it is, I'll act dumb.'* "No, he's either at OPD's downtown division, or at our hotel. Do we have a problem?" she suspiciously enquired. "I'm sorry to inform you that your husband, Watch Commander, Sergeant Riggs Wilburn was shot at your residence, this afternoon, sometime around 2:30 p.m. He was taken to the Holy Ones Hospital," he sympathetically conveyed.

Instinctively, her eyes stung with tears, "Dear Lord. No, no, no," she cried in disbelief. "How bad?" "He took one in his chest, and the other on his right arm.

Prior to contacting you, I received a text from our Captain Elijah Hurd, and he advised your husband was heading into surgery. He also mentioned that he'll be forwarding an update on his condition as soon as possible," he replied. Based on her abrupt reaction, Carol and Duke posed a series of questions, "What is it? Is it Nate? Is it Brock?" Somewhat disoriented, she pulled away from her cell phone and covered the speaker, "Riggs was shot this afternoon. I need to finish talking to this Detective. Give me a few minutes," she nervously replied. "Detective Wilburn, are you okay?" he asked. Wiping her eyes, "Yes, I'm sorry. What happened?" "We're still gathering the facts, but it appears your husband, son, and family dog walked in on a burglary in progress," he answered.

"What kind of weapon was he shot with?" "A 25 caliber." "Riggs normally carries his Glock 42. Did he have a chance to return fire?" "He got off three rounds. One bullet struck the shooter in the head, and he died at the scene. The other two rounds struck his accomplice in the mid and lower torso. Based on the first responder's evaluation, he thought it was incredible that he was able to utilize such tactics, especially, since he was losing a significant amount of blood. Goes to show, never underestimate someone's will and determination."

"Knowing my husband, he used his last ounce of strength to protect our son. You mentioned two suspects. How many were there?" "Three." "Did you catch the other #$@%^&*?" she upsettingly questioned. "No, but currently Patrol is following up on a number of leads." "Nate, my son, he's alright, isn't he?" "Yes." "How's Grady, our dog?"

"I'm terribly sorry. He died at the scene." "OH NO!!" she agonizingly cried out. "Detective Wilburn, you would've been extremely proud of him. Accordingly, after Riggs was shot, the shooter aimed his weapon at your son's head. Evidently, your dog sensed something was dreadfully wrong, and went into an attack mode, which initially saved his life. Specifically, his death caused a timely distraction that created an opportunity for Riggs to retrieve his backup gun that was fastened around his calf. With no time to spare, he efficiently returned fire, and killed the shooter. Afterwards, the second suspect attempted to grab his partner's gun, and was severely wounded. During the commotion, the last suspect, allegedly your boyfriend fled the scene," he explained.

"My what?" "That's what has been alleged." "Who called it in?" "Your son did, sort of. Understandably, he was fairly nervous. Instead of dialing 911, he called 411 - information. Nonetheless, the operator connected him to us. Additionally, Larry Jang, your neighbor, who lives across the street, heard the gunshots, and he also contacted us." "Detective Olson, could you give me a moment? I just finished having lunch with my sister and best friend. I need to inform them," she conveyed. "No worries." With her hands trembling and barely covering the speaker, "My nose is stuffed up. Does anyone have any tissue?" she anxiously asked.

"Right away," he snapped. "I have some," a caring stranger offered. Accepting her sympathetic gesture, "We appreciate it," Carol graciously said. Passing them to her, "Here you go, honey." After blowing her nose, "I'm speaking with a Detective Olson, from LAPD's Internal Affairs Division.

Again, this afternoon, Riggs was shot at our home, during a burglary in progress. Nate and Grady were also with him. Nate wasn't hurt, but Grady died at the scene," she emotionally stated. "How's Riggs?" Carol intensely asked. "He was struck twice, and rushed to the hospital. Altogether, there were three suspects. Riggs effectively eliminated one, who was going to kill Nate. The second was severely wounded, and the third ran off." "He's one of the toughest dudes I know. He'll make it," Duke assuredly stated.

"Thank GOD, Nate wasn't hurt. But Grady, our precious dog, helped saved both of their lives," she sobbed. "Based on what he described, I'm hoping Nate isn't severely traumatized, if so, he'll need some professional counseling." Heavily cringing, "When he was a kid, he was prone to nightmares. And Grady, who would've thought - old stubborn dog," she lamented. "I'll miss him for the rest of my life." Pointing at her cell, "You shouldn't keep the Detective waiting any longer," Carol advised. "Thanks for holding," she said. "No problem."

"Oooh, did you hear what happened?" one of the eavesdroppers whispered. "Yeah, she's got a (expletive) haystack at her house. Which reminds me, whenever we go house hunting, make sure we thoroughly inquire about the neighbors. We don't want to live next to a person who possesses violent tendencies." "Or someone whose completely bonkers," his friend added.

As Harri and Detective Olson continued, "I should also inform you of another troubling aspect. Prior to transporting your husband, he was falling in and out of consciousness.

Reportedly, he whispered to one our officers - *'It was Wilt.'* " "Are you positive that my husband said Wilt?" she worriedly asked. "Yes. In addition, when the first responders arrived, they interviewed your son, and he advised us of your marital status. He also corroborated your husband's allegation. Furthermore, one of the suspect's sprayed painted, in bright red, on your bedroom wall, *'Stupid @$+%#*.'* Detective Wilburn, I know your husband and son are heavily on your mind. We'll have plenty of time to discuss this later."

"Is there any substantial evidence to support Wilt's involvement? And how does Riggs know who I'm dating?" she quizzed. "As we speak, CSU (Crime Scene Unit), is dusting for latent prints. In regards to how your husband knew who you were seeing? That's not complicated," he plainly responded. "Detective, I'm getting off this phone and taking the first available flight." "Harriet, um, Detective Wilburn, I hope you don't mind me calling you by your first name." "Uh-uh." "Would you like me to pick you up at the airport?" he asked. "No, when I arrive, I'll take a cab directly to the hospital." "Have a safe trip." [*'Click'*].

Scrolling passed numerous text messages, she thought, *'Why hasn't Nate called me?'* Afterwards, she pressed speed dial #2, [Cell phone rang] *"Yeah?"* "Are you alright?" she precariously asked." "Dad's in surgery. Ugh! In our house, there's blood splattered everywhere! When the paramedics and Police arrived, they only gave me a few minutes to shower, change, and take a few of my belongings. Then, they told me to leave, because our home is now a crime scene?? Mom, your (expletive) boyfriend shot Dad, and he tried to kill me!!" he frenziedly shouted.

"Nate, nothing has been proven yet..." Heavily breathing, "Are you listening??!! You weren't there!!" he viciously roared. "I understand you're upset..." "Mom, don't talk down to me! I'm not one of your flunkies! Wilt was there! Even though, they were wearing ski masks, I heard him tell his friend, *'don't forget mommy's brat!'* If it wasn't for Grady and Dad, I would be dead! And Grady is dead!! Your Police friends also stopped me from burying him in the backyard!" he loudly cried. "No baby, they were right," she softly advised. "Whatever happened to all of your fancy talk about exercising good judgment? Huh?? Or was that just for everyone else? Dad could be dying, and I'm wasting my time talking to your (expletives)!" he furiously shouted.

"I'm so sorry. I didn't know," she pitifully cried. "When I first met the dude, I told you, he was bad news!" "Nate, I'm taking the next flight out. And don't call Nana or Grandma Wilburn, it'll only upset them. I'll get in touch with them, once I speak with his doctor." "Huh, I already spoke to Nana, and she said, *'See what sluts get for bed hopping.'* "I wished you hadn't. As usual, she doesn't know what in the hell she's talking about," she aggravatingly commented. "She's smarter than you!" he fired back. "I deserve that." "Which airport are you flying into? Burbank or LAX?" "Burbank. It's closer." [*'Click'*]. "Bye, son."

"Which airport?" Duke anxiously shouted. "OAK! (Oakland Airport). I'll connect with a shuttle to SFO (San Francisco)," she hastily replied. As they sprinted down the street, Harri's eye-catching scarf unraveled from around her neck, and landed on the ground.

Like clockwork, Carol scooped it up, and continued. Powerfully, jabbing the pedestrian's cross walk button, and inching beyond the curb, "Whose car is closer?" "Mines," Carol snapped. "Where is it?" Pointing down the street, "It's on the right hand side, see the white sedan?" ['Beep, Beep']. Afterwards, they rushed across the red light, and headed towards her vehicle. Remotely, she unlocked the doors, and Harri hopped into the front passenger's seat, while Duke climbed into the back. Zooming across numerous boulevards and streets, Carol was skillfully skipping through several traffic lights without incident. Approximately, two minutes later, she was radically swerving from rear ending another vehicle.

"Whoa that was close!" he terrifyingly stated as his body reflectively stiffened. "Lil sister, do you want me to drive?" "No." "Woo, you're driving like a bat out of hell!" he added. Glimpsing at Harri, "Since you were conducting business in Oakland, why didn't you fly directly into their airport?" she inquired. "I prefer United. So I took their route into San Francisco." Thereafter, she retrieved her cell phone and contacted the airlines, "This is Detective Harriet Wilburn, from the Southern Crest Police Department. I have a family emergency in Los Angeles County...."

Tapping her shoulders, "If you're on hold, hand me your keys, and I'll take care of your rental for you," Duke whispered. Retrieving and sliding them over her headrest, "Here they go." Spotting a near miss, "Carol, be careful!" she warned as she instinctively extended her left arm. "Hey, I know what I'm doing. In college, I used to drive for 'Buck-A-Buck Cab Service.'

Within six minutes, they were speeding on the Nimitz Freeway, I-880, heading Southbound to Oakland International Airport. "Right on, traffic is flowing!" she exclaimed. Discontinuing her telephone conversation, "United gave me two options. One flight leaves in an hour and twenty minutes, the other in two hours and ten minutes. And I still have to take a shuttle to SFO." Maneuvering into the carpool lane, Carol began inappropriately flashing her headlights, feverishly tailgating, and imploring some motorists to either speed up and/or move aside. "We'll arrive at OAK in ten minutes or less."

"Why is it that we don't appreciate our love ones until something tragic happens?" Harri tearfully asked. "It's called being human," he quietly responded. [Cell phone rang], "It's mines. This is Harri." "I just heard. Are you on your way back?" Brock sympathetically enquired. "Yes." "Babe, make sure you're flying directly into Burbank. You'll be closer." "I am. Who's taking my place?" "McNally. He left as soon as we got the news." "Brock, I don't feel well. Could I call you from the airport?" "Sure, we'll talk in a few, and don't worry about your clothes at the hotel. I'll pick those up." "Thanks." "Take it easy" ['Click'].

Contemplating her short-lived affair, *I thought Wilt at least liked me. How could I've been so wrong? I can't believe he betrayed me. And why would he want to kill Nate? He never did anything to him. This is surreal.'* Thereafter, she speed dialed his cell number. Glimpsing at her, "Who are you calling?" Carol distrustfully questioned. Shamefully nodding and disconnecting the line, "I changed my mind," she cagily replied.

Unpredictably, she started taking erratic, short, and rapid breaths. Clutching her dry throat, "I can't, I can't breathe," she madly cried. "Oh dear, you're hyperventilating. Duke somewhere back there, you should see a small brown paper bag, with two boxes of green tea inside, and a bottle of water rolling around on the floor." *'Good thing I didn't guzzle it all,'* he thought. "Got it!" Without delay, he handed her the small bag, and slid the half emptied water bottle beside her, "Clamp that over your mouth and nose, and take several deep breaths," he attentively instructed. As if her very life depended on it, she snatched it, and complied.

Shortly afterwards, she started breathing normally, as well as sipping some water, "I've never done that before." *'Your husband has never been shot before,'* he thought. Noticeably, Carol was seriously mumbling. "What are you saying?" Harri annoyingly inquired. "I'm praying. I know you and Duke aren't very religious," she answered. "Did you say one for Riggs?" "Naturally, he was first. I have faith everything will work out." "Lil sister, don't worry about my weak religious beliefs, do whatever you feel is best," he earnestly said. Continually, announcing their estimated time of arrival, "We should be there in less than five minutes," she assured.

Meanwhile in the back seat, Duke retrieved his cell phone and called his daughter, [Ring, Ring, Ring] "Hello." "Hi Rosa." "Hi Dad." "How's everything going?" he whispered. "Um, fine," she unevenly replied. "Are you upset?" "No, it's nothing." "It's something. What's wrong?" he worryingly asked. "I don't suppose to say," she reluctantly responded.

Taking a deep breath, "You know, you can tell me anything." "Not this. You'll get upset, and then, you'll call Mom." "That's what's bothering you? I promise I won't. If it's that important, I'm certain she'll contact me. Now what's going on?" he restlessly inquired. "Last night, Mom was on the phone speaking with Palo, and I overheard her saying that she'll 'consider moving to Ensenada.' Yesterday, he was arrested at work, and he might be getting deported. Dad, I don't want to move. This season, I'm joining the girls' basketball team, and I'm trying out for the cheerleaders next month. Could I live with you?" she sadly requested. "Darling, whenever you want. But you should know that legally your Mom can't relocate you out of California without my explicit consent, and that's not going to happen," he explained.

"Um hum." "Remember, your Dad wouldn't lie to you." Sniveling over the phone, "Okay." "Sweetheart, I'm heading into an important meeting, but I'll call you tomorrow morning before you leave for school. Don't worry. Have a terrific day. Love you." "I love you too. Bye." "Bye." *['Click']*. [Cell phone rang], "This is Duke." "Hey Sport, how's Central America?" Ross jovially asked. "Everything is fine, but I can't talk right now. I have a critical issue unfolding. Could I call you back?" he whispered. "I'll make it quick. Right now, we're in Seville, Spain. Since I couldn't sleep, I thought I would give you a ring-a-ling. Anyway, um, I was thinking about what we discussed before I left. After careful consideration, I don't believe adding a disco skating section with your existing business is a good idea. We can also quash our tentative partnership plans," he sheepishly said. "Fine," he agitatedly whispered.

"To be fair, Barbara (wife) insisted that I share with you my medical history." "Why?" "Dude, I'm bipolar and diabetic. I've also been diagnosed with PTSD (Post Traumatic Stress Disorder), Hypertension, and my doctor suspect that I maybe Schizophrenic. Don't be too alarmed there's over 40 million people nationwide who have a mental illness." "Ross, it's unbelievable that you withheld such vital information," Duke disturbingly stated. "Dude, it's not something you just willy-nilly discuss. Often times I feel great, so I'll skip my meds. However, whenever Barb finds out, I'm in deep horse pookie. Since I'm an open book, I should also reveal what's behind my decision.

While on holiday, I informed her of your proposal, and the possibility of a partnership. Once she ran the numbers, she torpedoed the whole freakin thing. She said, and I'll quote, *It stinks to high heaven!* " he frankly revealed. Completely blindsided, he temporarily lowered his cell. "Duke, baby, are you still with me? Hello, Hello! Did we get disconnected?" he apprehensively yelled. Finally, he lifted his phone, "Yep. I'm still here. Let me get this straight. So Barb approves some of your investments?" he flatly asked. "Heck no! She's responsible for rubber stamping all of them. Barbie is a mean machine, when it comes to business. Given my wobbly state of mind, I'm liable to agree with anything," he half-jokingly replied.

"Dude, I need to hang up. Call me late tonight, or tomorrow morning," he suggested. "It's after 1:00 in the morning here. How about if I call you two weeks from Sunday? Don't forget, I suppose to be spending quality time with the old ball and chain. Hey, don't tell her I said that.

Say Dukaroo, I hope you're not sore." "Forget it, man." "When we return, I'll treat for lunch – How does that sound?" he gleefully proposed. "Sure, Ross." *['Click']*. Gazing out of the rear passenger window, he irritatingly thought, *'Maya isn't crossing the border or moving my child anywhere. If she wants to trot around the globe after Palo, that's her darn business. Shoot. I should pick up my baby girl tonight. No, don't panic. I know I promised Rosa that I wouldn't contact her mom, but this is one, I can't possibly keep. I'll just have to apologize. And Ross, that man-child has talked me into some (expletive)!*

Barbara has been carrying his crazy ^!$%#@' all this time? Is this still Thursday afternoon? It feels like a whole week has whizzed by.'* Wiggling his left hand near her earlobe, "Harri, if you think you're done, give me that bag." Passing it over her shoulders, "It's all yours." "I may have another use for it," he grumpily muttered.

CHAPTER 11

<u>You Can't Unscramble the Eggs</u>

Four minutes later, a loud screeched was heard at the door steps of Oakland International Airport, and the front passenger's door swung wildly open. "I'm gone!" Hastily, climbing out of the driver's side, and racing towards the entrance, "Wait Harri!" Carol passionately yelled. Impatiently halting, "Hurry up." "Let me give you a hug before you go." Straightaway, they both hugged and kissed her. "Don't drive, because you've been drinking," Duke warned. "I won't." Holding up his cell, "If you need anything, call me," he added.

"As soon as I arrive home, Bonnie and I are flying up there. I'll also book a room near the hospital. I know you've got it altogether, but right now you need us," she encouraged. With tears irrepressibly flowing down her cheeks, "Um hum. I'll see you soon," she cried. Hugging her again, "You can count on it." Frantically, waving his hands and aiming at the sliding doors, "GO! GO!" As Harri sprinted, she unexpectedly pivoted, and appreciatively shouted, "Love you!" "Bye Harri, we love you too! Bye Sweetheart! With GOD's Speed!" they randomly echoed.

Sauntering towards her vehicle, "Lil sister, you've done a hell of a job driving. However, for the sake of keeping my undies halfway decent, could I wheel us home? You scared the bejeebers out of me," he half-jokingly conveyed. Dabbing perspiration from her face, "I could use a mental break. Duke, I have a confession to make."

"I don't think I can handle anymore," he quipped. "I hate fibbing. Essentially, I was never employed by a taxi service," she frankly admitted. "You could've fooled me." Opening the front passenger's side door, "So it was you?" "What are you referring to?" she asked. "I kept hearing the weirdest tapping noise, but I thought it was coming from Harri. Hum, I should've known. Are you ready?" "Um hum."

Meanwhile, in record time, Harri arrived at The Holy Ones Hospital, and noticed multiple squad cars scattered throughout the parking lot. Proceeding through the main entrance, she began recognizing and acknowledging many of her husband's colleagues from LAPD's Mission Hill's Station. Afterwards, she rushed to the front counter. In the midst of providing some pertinent information to the charge nurse, she saw a tall, string bean young fella, with light brown hair, briskly walking down the corridor; sporting a grey hoodie ensemble along with matching tennis shoes. Waving over head, "Nate!" she robustly shouted. Pivoting in her direction, "Mom!"

Promptly, he scurried over, and they tearfully hugged. "You got here fast. Dad just came out of surgery, and they placed him in the Intensive Care Unit (ICU). They won't let me see him, and the doctors hasn't come out yet," he pitifully cried. Wiping his face, "Listen, your Dad isn't leaving us - not today. You'll see," she assuredly said. "Are you alone?" "No, Linda is in the restroom." "Where were you headed?" "They have a small waiting room outside the unit. The nurse told us that we should stay in there." "You want to wait for Linda?" "No, she knows where it's located."

Wrapping her arm around his, they strolled to the designated area. "Mom, I'm sorry how I spoke to you, I..." he regretfully said. Leaning sideways and kissing his cheek, "Shhh, we all say things that we don't mean, especially whenever were under enormous stress. I'm sorry too." Near the doorway, she felt a mild tap on her shoulder from a short, young, blonde teenager, who wore a casual blue jean outfit, "Hi Mrs. Wilburn. Sorry about Mr. Wilburn," Linda respectfully stated. "It's nice seeing you again," she responded as they embraced.

"Could I get you something to drink? Coffee, water, or a diet soda?" she offered. "In the vending machine, they have that mango juice you like," he kindly mentioned. "No, I just want to wait for the doctor," she tensely responded. An hour and a half later, two male surgeons with white hair approached, and one softly inquired, "Mrs. Wilburn?" Popping out of her seat, "Yes. Is my husband alright?" "Good evening, I'm Dr. Haughton, your husband's surgeon. Sorry to meet you and your family under such circumstances. I know you're anxious to know his condition. So I'll get to the point. Your husband sustained one bullet wound that entered his chest, below his right collar bone. We were compelled to go in, and remove it," he responded. Cringing in a harsh manner, "That doesn't good," she uttered.

"There was also a second bullet that entered his right arm, and struck his brachial artery, which caused him to lose a considerable amount of blood. Presently, he's in critical condition, so we're keeping him in I.C.U for an undetermined length of time. To say the least, he has been through quite an ordeal."

Eyeing his colleague, "Hello, I'm Dr. Waterson, and I assisted Dr. Haughton during surgery. Mrs. Wilburn, I'm assuming the young man sitting next to you is your son?" he asked. "Yes, this is Nathan," she replied as she turned and peered at him. "Young man, you should be commended for your quick response." "No one told me anything," she confusedly mumbled. "Dad was bleeding a lot. Somehow I recalled my first aid training from Boy's Scout," he conveyed. "What did you do?" she asked. "First, I took off my shirt, and ripped it into two pieces. Then, I ran into the kitchen, grabbed a long wooden spoon, and built a tourniquet around his arm. Next, I went into the hall closet, snatched two large bath towels, and placed pressure on his other wound," he modestly replied.

Fiddling with his cellphone, "I kept saying, *The ambulance is coming. Hold on Dad.*" "The paramedics who brought your father in advised us of your actions. Indeed, the steps you took saved his life," Dr. Haughton added. "Now we have three heroes in our family," she proudly boasted. Patting him on his shoulder, "Good job," Linda said with a soulful glance. Afterwards, Harri sauntered towards him, leaned over, cupped his youthful face, and kissed him on the cheek, "I love you so much," she blissfully whispered. "Doctors, I can't thank you enough for everything you've done," she said while shaking both of their hands. Fondly, pointing to Nate's companion, "Before you leave, I would also like you to meet Linda. She's my son's girlfriend."

"Nice to meet you," they casually remarked. "You too," she politely said. "When can we see him?" Harri eagerly inquired. "Presently, he needs his rest. It'll be a few hours yet...," Waterson wisely advised.

"We're camping out here, if you need us." "Don't forget, you and your family should also get some sleep," he cautiously added. Retrieving her cell, "Nate, your Aunt Carol and Bonnie are supposed to be flying in." "That's cool. I haven't seen them in a long time. I'm glad they're coming." Two and a half hours later, they hurried inside, everyone hugged each other, and Nathan appropriately introduced Linda. "How's Riggs?" Carol nervously inquired. "He's in critical condition, and they haven't allowed us to see him yet."

Subsequently, Dr. Waterson walked in, "Mrs. Wilburn, your husband is temporarily awake. You and your family can go see him, but only for a couple of minutes." Immediately, everyone headed inside such unit. Then, Harri sharply halted, "You guys go first. I need to speak with him alone." "Sure, we understand," Carol said. "Nate, no matter how your father looks, try to remain calm." "I will." When they initially entered, one of the nurses raised her index finger and mimed, *You can only stay for a minute.* Of course, Carol readily understood.

As they approached, Riggs eyes were shut, right arm and upper torso were heavily bandaged, and a morphine drip was situated adjacent to his bed. Inching along his left side, "Dad, are you awake?" he meekly asked. With no response given, "Aunt Carol, Bonnie, and Linda are also with me." Seconds later, he provided a one sided grin. Then, unexpectedly, he slowly slid his left hand near his outer thigh. Obliging his father's loving gesture, Nate held his hand for a fleeting moment. "Love you Dad. I'll see you tomorrow. Get some rest," he tenderly whispered as a single tear fell onto his blanket.

Then, Carol and Bonnie stepped forward, "We love you brother," she softly said as she kissed the top of his forehead. Consequently, Bonnie experienced some emotional difficulties, and swiftly departed from the unit. Afterwards, Carol and Nathan met Bonnie standing outside the door. "Mom, Uncle Riggs wasn't breathing right, and he looked like he was in pain," she miserably said. Grabbing her hand, "Come on, you're tired. Let's get you something to eat." Lingering in the corridor, "How's he doing? Did he say anything?" Harri quizzed. "No, but Dad is really weak," he murmured. "We're going to find something to snack on. Do you want anything?" Carol asked. "Uh-uh. Did you book a room?" "Um hum, we're at the Shepherd's Inn."

Removing her wallet, "Nate, could you do me a favor? Take my credit card, and book us two rooms at the same place." "For how long?" "A week." "Harri, I also packed some extra clothing. Before you head to your room, stop by ours." "Okay." "Hey everybody, before I forget, don't buy any toothpaste. Yesterday, Scott's Dad gave us ten more cans. I left five at home, and the others are stashed in my trunk," he announced. Peeking at Carol, "Did you say toothpaste?" Harri gingerly asked. "Yeah, Scott's Dad is breaking into the dental industry. Isn't that awesome?" he gladly related. Subtly, winking at Harri, "Very nice," Carol said with a smirk. "Everyone looks pretty exhausted. You guys should shove off," she wisely stated.

"Are you certain you don't want me to stay here with you?" Carol asked. "I'm positive. I'll see Riggs for a couple of minutes, and then, I'll leave. I also need to pick up my truck from the airport."

"Mom, I could drop them off, then come back, and take you," he thoughtfully offered. "That's way too much driving. You guys go ahead. I need to be alone for a while, anyway. Tomorrow, we'll see each other either for breakfast or lunch." Prior to stepping away, "Try not to worry too much," Carol said. Subsequently, she pulled her near, and upsettingly whispered, "I'm so frighten. My hands won't stop shaking." "Harri, I have faith that GOD will see him through," she uttered as she kissed her on the cheek. Rejoining Bonnie, they waved farewell, "Bye Aunt Harri." "Mom, I'll text you with all of the hotel information. See you tonight. Let's go Linda."

Sauntering into the Intensive Care Unit, *'Lord, help me...,'* she mercifully prayed. Gradually, she walked inside and was tersely stopped by a nurse, "Only for a minute," she gently cautioned. From across the room, Harri observed his vulnerable condition. Lightly, biting her nails, *'For some reason, he looks much smaller,'* she fearfully thought. As she moved closer, involuntarily, her heart began pounding and her knees were knocking. Struggling emotionally and physically, she dared to take another step. Partially covering her mouth, she murmured, *'Oh Jesus.'* Bashfully, she stood next to his bed, and felt overwhelmed due to her troubling conscience. Then, she knelt, bowed her head, and silently prayed, *'In the name of the father, son, and the holy spirit. Lord, I willfully confess that I'm a sinner. I know you don't hear from me that often...'*

A few minutes later, she stood up, wiped her face, and daintily patted his left thigh, "Ri, Ri, Riggs, are you awake?" she fretfully stuttered.

Since his eyes were shut, and he failed to respond, she continued, "Your doctors advised that you needed plenty of rest. I won't stay long. I know I have no right to be here. I'm so sorry for everything." Gazing at the various high tech medical equipment, "You help me grow so much, but you left out the part about how I suppose to handle this," she tenderly cried. Faintly, shrugging her shoulders, "I don't know what else to say, except I royally screwed up. I never imagined that this would've happened. If I had the power, I would trade places."

Lowering her head, "I've never stopped loving you," she sorrowfully professed. "Sweetheart, please forgive me. I'll see you tomorrow, if that's alright with you." Prior to leaving his bedside, she delicately stroked his salt and peppered hair, and tenderly kissed his cheek. With her lips uncontrollably trembling near his earlobe, "Honey, I'm afraid. Don't leave us," she humbly implored. Heading towards the door, another nurse approached her, "Mrs. Wilburn?" "Yes." "We'll take good care of him," she generously whispered. Touching her hand, "Thank you so much."

Once she departed, and the door was closed, his eyes progressively opened, and he disturbingly thought, *'Yea, yea, I heard you. You're extremely sorry. But what you conveniently omitted is you're also responsible for killing Grady, my best buddy, and almost our son, our only child, over some lame (expletives)! If I wasn't lying here in such excruciating pain, I would've told the nurses to throw your pathetic, unconscious, (expletives) out of here.'* Consequently, he levelheadedly pondered over the recent chain of events, *'Harri, what happened to you?*

Whatever happened to my girl?' With the morphine drip situated nearby, he slowly retrieved the activation button, pressed it, and gloomily uttered, "I hate taking drugs."

Meanwhile actively wandering through the corridor, SCPD's Lieutenant Mark Janssen and Officer Mulligan, his aide, were searching for the ICU's waiting room, and Harri spotted them, "Lieutenant!" she shouted. Trotting over, "I really appreciate both of you coming." Rubbing the back of his neck, "How's your husband?" LT. Janssen softly asked. "He's in critical condition. After surgery, they placed him in the Intensive Care Unit. At this point, his doctors emphasized that he requires plenty of rest. Other than that, it's too soon to tell. Right now, he's sleeping," she answered. "We don't want to disturb him. We'll come back tomorrow afternoon. Are you the only one here?" he curiously asked.

"No, not really. A boat load of Police Officers from LAPD's Mission Hill Division as well as other personnel from nearby stations have been dropping by. I also heard the Chief of Police visited earlier. They've all been very kind. In addition, my son, his girlfriend, as well as my sister and niece from the Bay Area, left a few minutes ago. I was preparing to call a cab. My truck is at the airport," she answered. "We'll take you. We're in the department's van. You'll be more comfortable." "Are you sure?" she asked. "It's the least we could do." On route to the airport, "Did you happen to see Captain Randolph?" he asked. "No, I didn't." "I believed he arrived, when Riggs was being taken into surgery." "In actuality, this is our second visit.

Accordingly, your husband made a serious allegation, and we needed to follow up on it as soon as possible." "I know what that's all about," she embarrassingly mumbled. "In addition, I don't know if you're aware, the shooter died at the scene, and the second suspect DOA (dead on arrival), at the hospital. Earlier, we took fingerprints of both suspects, and they're currently being ran through the system. Nathan also stated he recognized one of the suspects. So we requested that he preview their bodies. Unfortunately, he didn't recognized either one," he casually mentioned.

Out of the blue, "How dare you involve my son??" she infuriatingly hollered. Whirling in his seat, "Calm down." "I will not!" "Have you've lost touch with reality?" he shouted. "Detective Wilburn, you've carefully planned, prepared, and cooked a hearty meal. Then, you discovered that you can't unscramble the eggs, and that makes me the (expletives)? I wasn't planning on crossing this bridge until next week. Could you please refrain?" he distressingly asked. Leaning aggressively forward, "My poor son was a helpless victim in this situation! Without a doubt, he has been dramatized from witnessing the shooting of his father, and the killing of Grady, our precious dog!" Mindlessly, pounding on the back of his seat, "Have you forgotten that he was also forced to act as a first responder?

Then, if that wasn't bad enough, you mercilessly subjected him to view the bodies of two cold-blooded hoodlums, who attempted to wipe out my entire family! Who in the (expletive) are you??!! What gives you the #@%^&* right??!!" she exhaustively cried.

Readjusting his seat, staring directly into her eyes, and using an authoritative voice, "Detective, your rage is sorely misplaced. Take it down, right now!!" Momentarily exhaling, "I understand you're hurting. Believe me, you and your family have our deepest sympathy. However, since you're forcing me to address this emotionally charged issue. So be it! Due to your callous indiscretion, you're principally responsible for the following: First and foremost, by no fault of his own, your husband was severely wounded, due to you secretly dating a felon, which is contrary to SCPD's rules and regulations. By all accounts, Riggs Wilburn is a well-respected Watch Commander and Sergeant of the Los Angeles Police Department.

Secondly, you have single handedly tarnished our hard earned reputation, as well as jeopardized our association with such department. I have you know, prior to you and your partner joining their task force, we assured them *'the best and the brightest'* would be assigned." Elevating his pitch, "They must think we're all psychotic!" he vehemently shouted. "Generally speaking, we handed them an irresponsible, reckless, rogue, female Detective. How disgraceful! Thirdly, you, and you alone, placed your son in this rather disheartening predicament, we didn't. In addition, for your information, presently there are two investigations concerning this matter," he said. "Why?"

"Isn't it obvious? The crime was committed within our jurisdiction, but it involves their officer. Lastly, due to such dire circumstances, I'll save our discussion on how you've adversely impacted your career for another day," he unambiguously stated.

Dismally, peering out of the rear window, *'Yes, but I'm a Mom first, and then, a peace officer,'* she thought. After thoroughly reflecting over his rational statement, "Sir, I truly apologize for my crude and vulgar outburst. I hope you can forgive me," she tearfully expressed. Studying the road up ahead, he deliberately failed to respond, but meditatively thought, *'I love my kids too.'*

CHAPTER 12

Starting Anew

Two and a half months later, a strong-featured, handsome, and considerably tall gentleman wearing an appealing dark blue sweat suit ensemble; along with a pricey pair of blue and gray tennis shoes, strolled into LAPD's Crenshaw Station. Specifically, he was cradling an adorable, small, brown and white, shaggy dog. As he proceeded to the information desk, a young Peace Officer, with a fresh crew cut readily approached. "Good afternoon sir, I'm Peace Officer Roberto Prieto. How may I help you?" he politely asked. "My wife is Detective Harriet Wilburn, with the Southern Crest Police Department. Do you know if she's still here?"

"Are you Sergeant Riggs Wilburn?" "Yes." Shaking his free hand, "Sir, it's a pleasure." Pointing in the appropriate direction, "Head straight down the hall, when you see the blue bulletin board, make a right. Then, pass two offices. She should be working in the third. Detective Wilburn and her partner have been conducting interviews for the better part of the morning." "Busy," he uttered. "Yes, sir." Afterwards, he promptly adhered to the explicit directions, silently entered the *'Observation Room,'* and stood near the doorway. Lifting the dog's left ear, "It looks like your Mom is interrogating a really bad dude," he jokingly whispered. "Shhh," someone snapped. "Sorry," he mimed. *'Wow, I didn't think anyone could hear me. And my buddy, could start yapping his head off at any moment. We better hang outside,'* he reasonably thought.

Fifteen minutes later, Harri departed, spotted her husband, and walked over. "Hi Gorgeous," he smoothly remarked. "Hi Honey," she lovingly responded as she planted one on his lips. "Is everything okay?" "Yes, I thought I would surprise you on your last day working with us." "How sweet. A few minutes ago, I received a text from Prieto saying you were in the observation room. Did someone request that you leave?" she strangely asked. "I was a bit noisy. Amazingly, my new pal was quiet as a church mouse." Rubbing his fluffy hair, "He's precious. What breed? And who does he belong to?" she casually quizzed.

"The lady at the shelter told me that he's mixed with a Yorkshire terrier, and that's all she knew. To answer your second inquiry, that's up to you." "What's his name?" "Accordingly, when one of the neighborhood kids brought him in, he wasn't wearing a name tag. Poor fella was discovered aimlessly wondering in an old junkyard. With only water in his bowl, and no food in sight, it was only a matter of time," he soberly replied. "You like him?" "Um hum. After some persuasion, the nice lady allowed me to borrow him for a few hours, so I could show him to you. Like I said, you have the deciding vote. Otherwise, I'm sold."

Scrutinizing his body, "He's so tiny, compared to Grady. Um, I don't know," she pessimistically expressed. "Honey, our Grady was a wonderful gift from GOD. Without a doubt, he bravely served his purpose, but he's gone now." "I know, you're right." Fondly, caressing him, "All this little fella wants is a loving family to share the rest of his life with." "Okay. If you ever take up a second career, don't become a used car salesman.

You had me thoroughly convinced, once you mentioned that he didn't have a morsel of food in his bowl." Spontaneously, [*'YAP! YAP! YAP!'*]. "Whoa! He's ferocious!" she joked. "Now you see why I chose him. He has a compact body, but a commanding bark. When I initially heard him, I had the same reaction, and I thought, *'Harri should see him.'* He's perfect for our family." "Yep, and since he's from the shelter, I have a unique name for him." "What is it?" he interestedly asked. "Shelby." Scratching his ears, "Did you hear that boy? Your name is Shelby. Sweetheart, could you skip out for lunch?" "Um hum. So far, I've only had a banana and some black coffee." "On my way here, I drove passed a new Deli. They also have a patio. You want to check it out?"

"Yeah. Give me ten minutes." Twenty five minutes later, she returned with her purse and jacket. "Ready," she said with a wide grin. With his right arm securely holding Shelby, and his left wrapped around her shoulders, they sauntered towards the exit. "This morning Captain Hurd texted me, and advised the Tijuana Police finally apprehended Wilt. Evidently, he crossed the border and shacked up with a young senorita. He also mentioned instead of waiting for the extradition process, we'll be picking him up this afternoon." "I'm sorry," she uttered. "Honey, I only told you, because eventually you'll have to testify in court. Otherwise, it's behind us." Gesturing with her right index finger, he bent downward, and she affectionately kissed him. Snuggling against his brawny chest, she thought, *'I have to ask.'* "Honey, why did you forgive me?

131

If the situation was reverse, I don't think I would've done the same." Admiring Shelby, "You're not the only one who fouled up. We both took turns driving our marriage off a cliff," he humbly acknowledged. "Were you also seeing someone?" she painfully asked. "I dated a pharmacist a few times. Nothing serious." With a scowl appearing across her face, "Was it Doreen? The blonde at Sloane's, who flirts with you every time we'd walked in there?" "Um hum." "That (expletive)! She couldn't wait to get her paws on you."

"You wanted me to be honest with you, right?" "So you forgave me, because it didn't work out with her?" she suspiciously questioned. "Uh-uh. Everything was fine. But after I was released from the hospital, I wanted to come home. So I told her it was over," he frankly explained. "Swell. Now I'll have to locate another pharmacy." "Why? Just kidding," he said with a chuckle. "There's plenty within a two mile radius." Taking a deep breath and exhaling, "I also called Mom." Rolling her eyes, "I can only imagine what she had to say." "Generally, I got the impression that she didn't feel it was appropriate to give any advice." "Incredible."

"However, before we hung up, she referred me to the Bible. Specifically, Mark, chapter eleven, verse twenty five thru twenty six," he answered. "Did you?" "Um hum." "What did it say?" "I'll let you read it for yourself." "Give me a hint." Gathering his thoughts, "I'll say this. After I read it, I prayed and asked for guidance, and concluded that I still love you. Generally, I also figured there were enough folks, who were out of practice. So I swallowed my pride, and accepted the responsibility."

Signaling for him to stoop down, they began kissing again. Grinning from ear to ear, "Sweetie, I still adore your luscious kisses," he whispered. "Mr. Shelby is also an affectionate dude. While we were necking, he was sneakily licking me on the side of my face. He is a boy?" she weirdly inquired. Chuckling out loud, "The last time I checked," he replied. As they continued strolling, "Before I forget, Duke sent us an email, and it said something like, *'Business is booming. Make sure to drop by, whenever you guys are in town.'* " "I'm wondering if he's referring to Plan A or B." "What's the difference?" he curiously asked. "I'll fill you in, once I speak with him."

"Perhaps this will help. He also attached a nutty photo of himself, presumably along with some of his guests and employees. They were dressed in 70's garb. You know, bell bottom pants and tight gaudy shirts." "Um hum." "In addition, everyone's hair were either styled straight and long, or into a humungous Afro. To top it off, they were all on roller skates." "That's fantastic!" "They looked as if they were having a ball," he said with a chuckle. "I can't wait to tell Carol. Speaking of which, early this morning, I talked with her on my way to work, and she said the company gave all of their employees a two percent pay increase." "Recently, our union negotiated for four. So two is better than nothing," he commented.

"Another upside is she's dating one of their Sport's Medicine Doctors." "Is that wise?" he prudently asked. "You mean dating a co-worker?" "Usually, those type of relationships have disaster written all over them, and they never last." "It should work out. Her shift starts early in the morning.

When she's done for the day, he's just arriving. During the week, they miss each other entirely, except, on the weekends. She also conveyed that he's charming, humorous, doesn't play games, or make her cry. Riggs, she never sounded happier," she satisfyingly stated. "In that case, they should be fine." "She also added Mason called last week, and said that he *'met the one.'* "That's great. He finally found someone special." "And Bonnie isn't acting out anymore. Apparently, Carol took Mister Man's advice, and reached out to Mrs. Daly, her High School Counselor, because her grades were slipping. In turn, she arranged for her to meet with Coretta, a popular youth counselor. She's also biracial as well as an honor student."

"How's that turning out?" he asked. "Wonderful. Carol said Coretta acts like her older sister." "Terrific. I'm delighted my niece is getting the help she needed." "Me too." "And you'll never guess what else." "Bet I can," he confidently said. "Alright big fella, go for it." "Eugene discovered the grass wasn't greener on the other side." "You talked with her?" "Uh-uh. I knew sooner or later, he would recognize that he messed up a good thing. When that occurs, most men have a tendency of trying to back track," he replied. "She won't take him back."

"I certainly wouldn't recommend it. Let him figure out his own foolish predicament – having a baby at his age. Whew! Based on everything that occurred within their marriage, it was time for her to move on," he earnestly determined. "My thoughts exactly." Midway towards the exit, he stopped, "I have something else for you. Look in my left pocket."

Quickly, she removed a white unsealed envelope, "Oh, goody another bill. I thought we've paid everything this month." "Open it." Patiently, he began observing her reviewing the contents. "Oooh wee! Two weeks in Paris! And we leave in six weeks!" "Did I get it right?" he modestly asked. "Yes, you did!" "The pushy travel agent tried to convince me to add other European cities, but I told him, *'Man, my wife will serve my head on a platter, if I screw this up.'* Right?" "Right! Finally, an honest to goodness vacation!"

Wiggling in place, "Let's not pack too much." "If you say so. By the way, are you free for dinner Friday night?" he kindly asked. Breaking out into a groovy twist, "Ooh-la-la!" "Madam, I'll take that as a yes. This evening, I'll confirm a time with Tom and Ellen." On a dime, she hastily stopped her happy dance. "Who are you referring to?" she asked in a disapproving tone. "The Barnett's – Linda's parents." "Ahh no, do we have to? I'm sure they think we're the worse parents in California." "I don't believe so. Last week, Tom and I briefly chatted over the phone. Understandably, they're disappointed, but he agreed somethings are out of the parent's control."

Exhibiting an awkward expression, "And if anyone were to back out, it should be them," he mumbled. "Hold up. I'm confused. What going on?" she disconcertedly asked. "Here's the deal. Before I left the house, Nate told me they broke up." Squinting her eyes, "He can't break up with her. She's pregnant!" "True..," he partially conveyed. "Huh, I know he didn't get that despicable move from my side of the family," she repulsively murmured. "Harri, I heard you, and that wasn't a very nice thing to say.

You should allow me to finish, before you rush in. It seems Nate was eliminating all of Linda's personal information on her old cell, prior to her purchasing a new one. Somehow he stumbled across some racy text messages from another fella," he explained. "EEK! There goes my big mouth again. Sorry, Riggs. Did he show them to you? Are they horrible?" she anxiously quizzed. "Rated X." "What's the timeline?" "Over three months." "Does her parent's know?" Shrugging his manly shoulders, "Beats me," he snapped. "And you still believe we should go out with them?"

"Yes, regardless of the outcome, we should remain supportive. Remember, our son slept with their daughter." "Is he going?" "Oh, he's going alright," he determinedly responded. "I'll make sure he wears a suit," she said. With an astonished gaze, "Why? The jig is up. Let him dress the way he wants to. I'll probably wear blue jeans and a sweat shirt." "Suppose the Barnett's try to persuade him or us that they should get married?" she asked. "If that subject comes up, let Nate and I address it. You'll get too worked up. Clearly, at this point, they're not holding the trump card." "I just don't want him to feel trapped, like you did," she mumbled.

"Girl, I would've never asked you to marry me, if I didn't love you." "No?" "After our first year, I heavily considered that we possessed several things in common. Neither one of us frequent night clubs, so I didn't have to worry that you'll meet another dashing guy the following weekend," he said, laughing. In addition, I also realized that we enjoyed the gym, same foods, movies, concerts, sports, car shows, as well as shared the same financial goals, and religious beliefs.

More importantly, we didn't quarrel that often. I also spoke with Dad," he answered. "And?" "As expected, a man of few words simply said, 'About time.' "Good ol' Dad." "Harri, I've told you this story at least four times. You just want to hear it again." "Maybe." "Didn't you find it peculiar once you revealed that you were pregnant, I immediately popped the question?" "I summed it up to gallantry," she smugly replied. "I had already purchased your ring. It was resting on top of my dresser. I was just gathering enough nerve to ask you. Your announcement made it easier," he convincingly said. Widely grinning, "Okay honey, this time, I believe you."

"Since we're playing truth or dare, I might as well lay this on you. Nate is mulling over the idea of joining the service, either the Army or Navy." Frantically, shaking her hands, "No, no, no." Glimpsing at her reaction, "This is exactly why he hasn't run it past you. His rationale is the military will pay for his college education. He told me in confidence. So don't say anything. Let him approach you, he will." "Ugh! This is too much to digest," she unsatisfyingly expressed. Heading towards the exit, "I've been meaning to ask you something." "What is it?" "How do you like that new toothpaste in a can?" "Never tried the stuff," he dryly answered. "Son-of-a-(expletive)!" Narrowing his eyes, "Don't tell me. You've been using that rubbish all this time?" he distressingly asked. "Um hum. I thought we all were." "Some time ago, I told Nate to get rid of that junk. Dave (Scott's Dad), don't know what in the hell he's doing, and I'm certain he hasn't been approved by the ADA (American Dental Association). For Pete's sake, he's an Express Mail Courier.

That slop, recycled poop, or whatever in the hell are in those cans, represents another one of his screwy concoctions. Boy, I hope he isn't slowly poisoning the whole darn neighborhood. If so, he could be arrested for several counts of second degree murder, manslaughter, or whatever the D.A.'s (District Attorney's) office determines," he stated. Descending from the top of the exterior staircase, she began frantically poking around her gums, grimly spitting on the ground, and swiping the edges of her mouth. *'Gee whiz, just when things were starting to look up,'* she irritatingly thought.

GLOSSARY

Al Jarreau (1940-2017): Alwin Lopez "Al" Jarreau was an American jazz singer and musician. He received a total of seven Grammy Awards.

Alcohol Anonymous (1935-Present); Alcoholics Anonymous is an international mutual aid fellowship founded in 1935 by Bill Wilson and Dr. Bob Smith in Akron, Ohio. AA's stated "primary purpose" is to help alcoholics "stay sober and help other alcoholics achieve sobriety."

American Dental Association (1859-Present): The A.D.A is an American professional association established in 1859 which has more than 155,000 members. Based in the American Dental Association Building in the Near North Side of Chicago,

Baby Boomers: (1946-1964): Baby boomers represents approximately 76.4 million people who were born following World War II, when there was a temporary marked increase in the birth rate.

Bellevue (1736-Present): Bellevue Hospital, was founded on March 31, 1736 and is the oldest public hospital in the United States. In 1876, they established the nation's first emergency pavilion. Specifically, a pavilion for the insane—an approach considered revolutionary at the time—was erected within hospital grounds in 1879. For this reason the name "Bellevue" is sometimes used as a metonym for psychiatric.

Beretta M9 (1985-Present): The Beretta M9, officially the Pistol, Semiautomatic, 9mm, M9, is the designation for the Beretta 92FS semi-automatic pistol by the United States Armed Forces. The M9 was adopted by the United States' military as their service pistol in 1985.

Bipolar Disorder (previously known as Manic Depression): Bipolar disorder is a mental disorder that causes periods of depression and periods of elevated mood. During mania, an individual behaves or feels energetic, abnormally happy, or irritable. Individuals often make poor decisions with little regard to the consequences.

Blue Chip Stamps: (1963-2011): Blue Chip Stamps started as a trading stamps company called "Blue Chip Stamp Co." They were a competitor to S&H Green Stamps. Blue Chip stamps were a loyalty program for customers, similar to discount cards issued by pharmacies and grocery stores in the digital era.

Boeing 777 (1995–Present): The Boeing 777 is a family of long-range wide-body twin-engine jet airliners developed and manufactured by Boeing Commercial Airplanes. It is the world's largest twinjet.

Burl Ives (1909-1995): Burl Icle Ivanhoe Ives was an American singer and actor of stage, screen, radio and television. He began as an itinerant singer and banjoist, and launched his own radio show, The Wayfaring Stranger, which popularized traditional folk songs such as *'Down in The Valley.'*

Chino State Prison (1941-Present): California Institution for Men is a male-only state prison located in the city of Chino, San Bernardino County, California.

City of Berkeley Police Department (1909–Present): The Berkeley Police Department (BPD) has over 170 sworn officers, and serves 17.9 square miles. Currently, the Chief of Police is Andrew Greenwood.

City of Los Angeles Police Department (1869-Present): The Los Angeles Police Department (LAPD), officially the City of Los Angeles Police Department, is the law enforcement agency for the city of Los Angeles, California, United States. It is the third-largest municipal police department in the United States. The department has approximately 10,000 sworn officers and serves an area of 498 square miles. Currently, Charlie Beck is the Chief of Police.

City of Oakland Police Department (1853-Present): The Oakland Police Department has 740 sworn officers, and patrols 55.9 square miles within Alameda County. Currently, Anne Kirkpatrick is Chief of Police.

Disco Dancing (Late 1960's - early 1980's): Disco is a genre of dance music containing elements of funk, soul, pop and salsa. It achieved popularity during the mid-1970s to the early 1980s.

Elvis Presley (1935-1977): Elvis Aaron Presley was an American singer, musician, and actor. Regarded as one of the most significant cultural icons of the 20th century, he is often referred to as the "King of Rock and Roll."

Federal Aviation Administration: (1958-Present): The Federal Aviation Administration of the United States is a national authority with powers to regulate all aspects of civil aviation.

Fred Jordan's L.A. Mission: (1944-Present): The Reverend Fred Jordan, whose Skid Row mission located in downtown Los Angeles feeds 1,000 people a day, along with clothing, blankets, and other vital services. Reverend Jordan was also a pioneer television minister whose "Church in the Home" was first broadcast in 1951.

Glock 42: The new GLOCK 42, in .380 AUTO, is a slim line subcompact pistol engineered with the GLOCK Perfection promise and able to withstand the rigors of routine training. Made in the USA, the G42 is the smallest pistol GLOCK has ever introduced.

Hollywood Burbank Airport - formerly Bob Hope's Burbank Airport **(1930-Present):** The airport serves the northern Greater Los Angeles area, including Glendale, Pasadena, and the San Fernando Valley.

Hound Dog Song (1952-Present): "Hound Dog" is a twelve-bar blues song written by Jerry Leiber and Mike Stoller. Recorded originally by Willie Mae "Big Mama" Thornton on August 13, 1952. "Hound Dog" was Thornton's only hit record. Elvis Presley also performed and featured such song on his album.

Karma (Pre 19th Century–Present): It's a Sanskrit word meaning 'act', 'action', or 'word'. The law of karma teaches us that all of our thoughts, words and actions begin a chain of cause and effect, and that we will personally experience the effects of everything we cause.

Leave It To Beaver (1957-1963): *Leave It to Beaver* is an American television sitcom about an inquisitive and often naïve boy.

Theodore "The Beaver" Cleaver (portrayed by Jerry Mathers), and his adventures at home, in school, and around his suburban neighborhood.

Manic Depressive: Alternating moods of abnormal highs (mania) and lows (depression). Called bipolar disorder because of the swings between these opposing poles in mood.

Mirandized (1966-Present): The concept of "*Miranda* rights" was enshrined in U.S. law following the 1966 *Miranda v. Arizona* Supreme Court decision, which found that the Fifth and Sixth Amendment rights of Ernesto Arturo Miranda had been violated during his arrest.

National Football League (1920-Present): The National Football League (NFL)) is a professional American football league consisting of 32 teams, divided equally between the National Football Conference and the American Football Conference.

National Enquirer (1926-Present): The National Enquirer (also commonly known as the Enquirer) is an American supermarket tabloid published by American Media Inc. (AMI).

Oakland International Airport (1927-Present): Oakland International Airport is an international airport in Oakland, California, United States. It is located approximately 10 miles south of downtown, and it's owned by the Port of Oakland.

Pacific Gas & Electric (1905-Present): Pacific Gas & Electric (PG&E) is an investor-owned electric utility (IOU) with publicly traded stock.

Papier-mâché (14th Century – Present): Papier-Mâché (commonly spelled as "Paper Mache") is a composite material consisting of paper pieces or pulp, sometimes reinforced with textiles, bound with an adhesive, such as glue, starch, or wallpaper paste.

Perry Mason (1933-Present): Perry Mason is an American fictional character, a criminal defense lawyer, who is the main character in works of detective fiction written by Erle Stanley Gardner. Perry Mason is featured in more than 80 novels and short stories, most of which involve a client's murder trial.

Peter White (1954-Present): Peter White is a smooth jazz and jazz fusion guitarist. He also plays the accordion and the piano. He is known for his 20-year collaboration with Al Stewart.

Platform Shoes: (15ᵗʰ Century – Present): Platform shoes are shoes, boots, or sandals with an obvious thick sole, usually in the range of 3–10 cm (1–4 in). Platform shoes may also be high heels, in which case the heel is raised significantly higher than the ball of the foot.

Post-Traumatic Stress Disorder (1980-Present): Post-Traumatic Stress Disorder (PTSD) is a disorder that develops in some people who have experienced a shocking, scary, or dangerous event.

Salvation Army (1865-Present): The Salvation Army is a Protestant Christian Church and an international charitable organization. The denomination reports a worldwide membership of over 1.5 million. Its founders Catherine and William Booth sought to bring salvation to the poor, destitute, and hungry by meeting both their "physical and spiritual needs." It is presently in 128 countries, operating charity shops, shelters, and humanitarian aid.

Smith & Wesson .40 Caliber (1990-Present): The .40 S&W is a rimless pistol cartridge developed jointly by major American firearms manufacturers Smith & Wesson and Winchester.[

Studebaker (1852-1967): Studebaker was an American wagon and automobile manufacturer based in South Bend, Indiana. Founded in 1852 and incorporated in 1868 under the name of the Studebaker Brothers Manufacturing Company, the company was originally a producer of wagons for farmers, miners, and the military.

The Bible (1300– 1500 BC): The Bible was written over a period of 1400 to 1800 years by more than 40 different authors. The New Testament (containing 27 books). It is believed all of the books of the Bible were written under the inspiration of the Holy Spirit.

The Humane Society of the United States (1954-Present): The Humane Society of the United States is the nation's largest and most effective animal protection organization. It is also an American nonprofit organization, and its efforts are to address animal-related cruelties on a national scope.

Transportation Security Administration (TSA): (2001-Present): The Transportation Security Administration is an agency of the U.S. Department of Homeland Security that has authority over the security of the traveling public in the United States.

Twenty Five Caliber -.25 ACP: (1905-Present): The .25 ACP (Automatic Colt Pistol) (6.35×16mmSR) is a semi-rimmed, straight-walled centerfire pistol cartridge introduced by John Browning in 1905.

"Type A" Personality Theory: "Type A" personalities are more competitive, highly organized, ambitious, impatient, highly aware of time management and/or aggressive.

United Airlines (1926-Present): United Airlines, Inc., commonly referred to as United, is a major American airline headquartered in Chicago, Illinois.

United States Army: (1775-Present): The United States Army (USA) is the largest branch of the United States Armed Forces and performs land-based military operations. It is one of the seven uniformed services of the United States and is designated as the Army of the United States in the United States Constitution.

University of Berkeley (1868-Present): UCB or Cal Berkeley is a public research university in Berkeley, California. Founded in 1868, Berkeley is the flagship institution of the ten research universities affiliated with the University of California system.

Upper Rockridge (Oakland, CA): Rockridge is a residential neighborhood and commercial district in Oakland, California.

Rockridge is generally defined as the area east of Telegraph Avenue, south of the Berkeley city limits, west of the Oakland hills.

Wikipedia (2001-Present): Wikipedia is a free online encyclopedia with the aim to allow anyone to edit articles. Wikipedia is the largest and most popular general reference work on the Internet and is ranked among the ten most popular websites. Wikipedia is owned by the nonprofit "Wikimedia Foundation."

Winchester Rifle (1866-Present): Winchester rifle is a comprehensive term describing a series of lever-action repeating rifles manufactured by the Winchester Repeating Arms Company. Developed from the 1860 Henry rifle, Winchester rifles were among the earliest repeaters. The Model 1873 was particularly successful, being colloquially known as *"The Gun that Won the West."*

Made in the USA
San Bernardino, CA
10 November 2019